Cookie Craft Christmas

DOZENS OF DECORATING IDEAS
for a Sweet Holiday

Valerie **PETERSON** *& Janice* **FRYER**

Storey Publishing

The mission of Storey Publishing is to serve our customers by publishing practical information that encourages personal independence in harmony with the environment.

Edited by Margaret Sutherland
Art direction and book design by Alethea Morrison
Text production by Jennifer Jepson Smith

Photography by © Kevin Kennefick, except back cover by Mars Vilaubi
Food styling by Sara Neumeier
Photo styling by Alethea Morrison
Illustrations by Alison Kolesar

Printed in China by SNP Leefung Printers Limited
10 9 8 7 6 5 4 3 2 1

Library of Congress Cataloging-in-Publication Data

Peterson, Valerie.
  Cookie craft Christmas / by Valerie Peterson and Janice Fryer.
    p. cm.
  ISBN 978-1-60342-440-0 (hardcover w/ jacket : alk. paper)
  1. Cookies. 2. Cake decorating. 3. Holiday cookery.
  I. Fryer, Janice. II. Title.
TX772.P453 2009
641.8'654—dc22
                                                        2009023709

ACKNOWLEDGMENTS

Cookie Craft Christmas owes a huge debt to the many of our beloved family members and friends whose generous support and enthusiasm helped us launch the original *Cookie Craft*. We thank you all, again, from the bottom of our mixing bowls!

The book owes its existence to our agent Jen Griffin and the wonderful team at Storey Publishing — especially our editor, Margaret Sutherland, and the creative director, Alethea Morrison. We're thrilled to be working once again with the amazing Storey sales and marketing teams and with Amy Greeman and Jayme Hummer in publicity. Thanks to them, we're catching up to "zucchini" . . . Dan knows what we mean.

We again thank our illustrator, Alison Kolesar, and our talented stylist Sara Neumeier, who, despite her best efforts, can't seem to escape us — for that, we're very grateful. And we're grateful, too, to Kevin Kennefick, our photographer, who shot the cookies in their best light.

Last but not least, we'd like to thank all our *Cookie Craft* readers and the numerous baking bloggers who've been so generous with their praise and helpful with their comments. Our "Easy" cookie icon and "Keep It Simple" notes came about as a direct response to reader feedback. We continue to be inspired by their creativity and enthusiasm!

CONTENTS

introduction

We wrote in our first book, *Cookie Craft*, that beloved memories are made and kept in the kitchen. Never is this truer for many of us than when making Christmas cookies.

At this most wonderful time of the year, Janice's mom, Mildred, always made Russian tea cakes. Valerie's mom, Weenie, hauled out the spritz cookie press, and the Petersons still laugh about the time the family dog ate an entire baking sheet of raw cookie dough. We both enjoy baking and eating traditional holiday recipes, but now our cherished traditions include decorating seasonal cookies. Many of our friends and families have gotten into the habit, as well, and their kids look forward to the annual ritual.

Janice makes her much-requested snowflakes for the office holiday potluck and loves to give elaborately decorated cookies as special gifts. Valerie makes trucks with trees as an emblem of her family's annual "Tree Day," when her freshly cut evergreen actually leaves the tree farm on her cousin Kurt's red pickup.

While writing and decorating for the year-round *Cookie Craft,* we realized we could fill a whole book with just Christmas shapes — each one in its own way a treasured symbol of the season — and the idea for this follow-up was born.

Here, in *Cookie Craft Christmas,* you'll find more than 70 unique holiday cookies, as well as our favorite recipes, shortcuts, hints, tips, and detailed instructions for how to achieve the results pictured. Use the ideas as jumping-off points for your own creativity, and have fun putting your personality into the cookies. For many of the designs, we suggest ways to "Keep It Simple" — that is, how to get a similar result with fewer steps or less drying time. In response to our readers, we've also included simpler cookie designs for beginners or for quicker decorating gratification for anyone. You'll find these flagged with an "Easy" icon. (For additional techniques, more in-depth beginner instruction, and year-round inspirations, you can of course refer to the original *Cookie Craft.*)

Though the holiday season is always busy, making time for tomorrow's memories has never been more important. We hope this book helps to make your Christmas cookie crafting merry and your baking season bright!

recipes & techniques

first things first: making cookies

All of our Cookie Craft Christmas creations start with delicious sugar cookies, yummy gingerbread, or rich chocolaty cookies. We developed the recipes and the rolling-chilling-cutting technique here to ensure a smooth surface for your successful holiday designs. Be sure to check out the Pre-baking Decorating Techniques (page 12) for easy ways to embellish your cookies before they go into the oven. Many of the more elaborate designs here are made with royal icing; if you've never used it before, we give you recipes and handy hints (pages 15–21) to ensure your decorating fun.

EQUIPMENT

While you can decorate cookies with not much more than basic baking supplies, a plastic bag, and a batch of royal icing, the following inexpensive equipment will make your cookie decorating more efficient and fun. See Resources for suppliers.

* *waxed paper* — for quick and easy rolling/chilling/cutting.

* *cookie slats* — for perfectly even cookies (see page 9).

* *rolling pin* — you probably have one on hand.

* *cookie cutters* — a round biscuit cutter is versatile; we use it in a number of designs.

* *parchment paper* — for easy stick-free cookie baking

* *2-cup airtight plastic containers* — to store royal icing.

* *pastry bags* — for piping royal icing. In a pinch, you can use a quart-size ziplock freezer bag. Insert the coupler and tip in one corner of the bag (as instructed on page 21). No coupler and tip? Cut the tiniest hole possible in the corner of the bag, which will give you a similar effect to using a #2 tip.

* *metal decorating tips* — a #2 tip is very useful.

* *plastic decorating tip couplers* — makes changing tips easy.

* *twist ties* — useful for closing pastry bags.

* *plastic squeeze bottles* — for flood icing.

* *small paintbrushes* — for luster dust.

ROLLED SUGAR COOKIES

Yield

2½-inch cookies: about 30

3½-inch cookies: about 16

4½-inch cookies: about 12

Ingredients

3 cups all-purpose flour

½ teaspoon salt

1 cup (2 sticks) unsalted butter, softened

1 cup sugar

1 large egg

2 teaspoons vanilla* or 1 teaspoon vanilla plus zest of 1 lemon

food coloring (if your cookie design calls for it)

* Instead of vanilla, you can use other extracts such as almond or peppermint, which we like for candy-cane shapes. If you're going to be decorating with royal icing, make sure the cookie and icing flavorings are complementary.

1 Whisk together the flour and salt in a medium bowl.

2 Cream together the butter and sugar with your mixer until light and fluffy. Add the egg, vanilla, and lemon zest (if you're using it) and mix until well blended.

3 With the mixer on low, gradually add the flour mixture to the butter mixture until the two are thoroughly blended. If your design calls for adding food coloring, do so now, and blend well.

4 Turn the dough onto a work surface and divide into two or three equal portions. Form each one into a rough disk. Now you're ready to roll, chill, and cut out cookie shapes. Find complete rolling and cutting instructions on page 9.

5 Preheat the oven to 350°F.

6 After you've rolled and cut the dough and the cookie shapes are on parchment-lined cookie sheets, bake them in the middle rack of your oven for 12 to 16 minutes or until the cookies start to turn slightly golden around the edges.

7 Cool the cookies completely before icing or decorating.

ROLLED CHOCOLATE COOKIES

Try these cookies any time you desire a chocolate-flavored cookie or a darker background for your decorative genius.

Yield

2½-inch cookies: about 30
3½-inch cookies: about 16
4½-inch cookies: about 12

Ingredients

2½ cups all-purpose flour
½ cup cocoa powder, either
  alkalized (Dutch-process) or
  natural (nonalkalized)
1 teaspoon instant espresso
  powder (optional but
  recommended)
½ teaspoon salt
1 cup (2 sticks) unsalted
  butter, softened
1 cup sugar
1 large egg
1 teaspoon vanilla

1   Whisk together the flour, cocoa powder, espresso powder, and salt in a medium bowl.

2   Cream together the butter and sugar with your mixer until light and fluffy. Add the egg and vanilla and mix until well blended.

3   With the mixer on low, gradually add the flour mixture to the butter mixture until the two are thoroughly blended.

4   Turn the dough onto a work surface and divide into two or three equal portions. Form each one into a rough disk. Now you're ready to roll, chill, and cut out cookie shapes. Find complete rolling and cutting instructions on page 9.

5   Preheat the oven to 350°F.

6   After you've rolled and cut the dough and the cookies are on parchment-lined cookie sheets, bake them on the middle rack of your oven for 12 to 16 minutes or until the cookies start to turn a deeper brown around the edges.

7   Cool the cookies completely before decorating.

ROLLED GINGERBREAD COOKIES

These cookies have a mild gingerbread flavor, and they make the kitchen smell wonderful while they're baking.

Yield

2½-inch cookies: about 48
3½-inch cookies: about 37
4½-inch cookies: about 18

Ingredients

5 cups all-purpose flour
2 teaspoons ground ginger
1 teaspoon ground cinnamon
1 teaspoon ground cloves
½ teaspoon baking soda
½ teaspoon salt
zest of 1 orange (optional)
1 cup (2 sticks) unsalted butter, softened
1 cup sugar
1 large egg
1 cup molasses

1 Whisk together the flour, ginger, cinnamon, cloves, baking soda, salt, and orange zest (if you're using it) in a medium bowl.

2 Cream together the butter and sugar with your mixer until light and fluffy. Add the egg and molasses and mix until well blended.

3 With the mixer on low, gradually add the flour mixture to the butter mixture until the two are thoroughly blended.

4 Turn dough onto a work surface and divide into three equal portions. Form each one into a rough disk. Now you're ready to roll, chill, and cut out cookie shapes. Find complete rolling and cutting instructions on page 9.

5 Preheat the oven to 350°F.

6 After you've rolled and cut the dough and the cookies are on parchment-lined cookie sheets, bake them on the middle rack of your oven for 12 to 16 minutes or until the cookies start to turn a deeper brown around the edges.

7 Cool the cookies completely before decorating.

READY TO ROLL: ROLLING, CUTTING, AND BAKING DOUGH

We use two pieces of waxed paper and two wooden strips we call cookie slats to roll out our dough before it is chilled. This method has many advantages:

The rolled dough is a perfectly even thickness (ensuring smooth, uniform cookies); it chills quickly for cutting; and you don't need to use extra flour to prevent the dough from sticking (it won't stick to the waxed paper), so your dough doesn't get dry. Any smooth kitchen surface will do for rolling cookies when you follow these simple steps. Lining your cookie sheets with parchment paper will prevent sticking and facilitate cleanup — we highly recommend it.

> ### COOKIE SLATS
>
> ✳ ✳ ✳ ✳ ✳ ✳ ✳ ✳ ✳ ✳ ✳ ✳ ✳ ✳ ✳ ✳ ✳
>
> *Cookie slats aren't mandatory, but we highly recommend using them to help you create cookies of a uniform thickness. You'll need two wood strips that are ¼ inch thick, 2 feet long, and 2 inches wide. They're sometimes called lattice slats or lumber scants, and are sold in hardware or craft stores for about $2 each – a small price to pay to speed your cookie rolling!*

1 Place a piece of waxed paper about the size of your cookie sheet on your rolling surface.

2 Place cookie slats on the edges of the paper. The slats should be a rolling-pin width apart, to ensure that there's stable contact between the slats and both ends of the rolling pin.

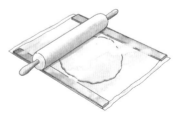

Using slats to roll out dough

3 Place a disk of cookie dough on top of the waxed paper, between the slats. Place another sheet of waxed paper over the cookie dough and slats and use your hand or rolling pin to slightly flatten and evenly distribute the dough across the paper. Roll the pin over the waxed paper-covered dough, making sure the ends of the pin stay on the slats as the dough flattens (the pin will hover above the slats at first).

If the top paper wrinkles, lift and smooth it. You're finished rolling when the dough surface is uniform and completely level with the cookie slats. You'll recognize this point: rolling the pin over the dough will feel effortless.

4 Slide the rolled-out piece of dough (paper and all) onto a cookie sheet and refrigerate until it's firm, 20 to 30 minutes. Repeat the rolling process with the remaining dough portions.

5 When the dough is firm and stiff, transfer it from the refrigerator to your flat work surface. Work with one piece of dough at a time, leaving the others to chill in the refrigerator until you're ready to cut them. Peel back the top waxed paper from the dough and cut your desired shapes. Try to get as many cookies as possible out of each rolled-out piece of dough.

6 Remove excess dough from around the shapes. Transfer the cookies to a parchment-lined cookie sheet.

7 When you've cut as many cookies as possible from all your rolled dough, gather the dough scraps into a ball and roll it again, using the same waxed-paper method. Continue to cut cookies and reroll the dough until you've used all the dough, chilling the rolled-out dough whenever it becomes too sticky to work with.

8 If you're using any of the prebaking decorating methods (imprinting, sugaring, add-ons, and so on), now's the time to get decorating.

9 Bake and cool the cookies as directed in the recipes.

FREEZING UNDECORATED COOKIES

✳ ✳

✳ *At cookie-decorating crunch-time just before the holidays, baking ahead and freezing ensures that your cookies will be ready when you have time to decorate.*

✳ *To freeze baked undecorated cookies, layer them in a flat, sturdy, covered container with waxed paper between the layers. (We do not recommend freezing decorated cookies.) To thaw your cookies for decorating, remove them from the freezer and place them in a single layer on cookie sheets. When they have reached room temperature, they're ready to decorate.*

prebaking decorating techniques

The cookie crafter's repertoire should include the gamut of easy, versatile prebaking techniques. From imprinting to add-ons, these techniques can be used in combination with royal icing or by themselves to create beautiful, whimsical, or just plain fun cookie designs.

IMPRINTING BEFORE BAKING

Imprinting your cookie dough before baking — that is, pressing designs into the raw dough — creates visual interest or highlights cookie features. We've used spatulas, toothpicks, drinking straws, and a variety of other household items to create particular imprinted designs. For example, you can use the blade of a small knife to mark lines on a holly leaf, like those on page 33.

MAKING HOLES OR CUTOUTS

Perforating your cookies is a simple technique that delivers a wide range of effects. Little round holes are useful for "stringing" an ornament or Christmas lights, and fancier shapes add interest to snowflakes. Use a plastic drinking straw to punch circles in unbaked dough. Sets of tiny aspic cutters come in shapes that broaden your cutout options (see Resources).

MAKING WINDOWPANES

Add crushed candies to your cutouts and you'll have windowpanes, which give your Christmas cookies a beautiful, see-through stained-glass effect. To crush hard candies, place them in a double-layer ziplock bag and smash them with a hammer until they're powdery or in tiny shards. Completely fill the holes in the cookie dough with candy. Bake the cookies according to recipe instructions; the candy will melt to create windowpanes. Cool the cookies completely on the cookie sheet before removing to allow the melted candy to harden.

COLORING DOUGH

Generally speaking, adding supermarket liquid food coloring to cookie dough will yield softer colors. Gel or paste food coloring from a baking specialty shop (see Resources) will give you more saturated, vibrant colors. Whichever coloring you use, add just a drop at a time — you can always add more, but you can't take away!

ADDING DIMENSION TO COOKIES

Add a second layer of dough detail to your base cookies to create dimension. To achieve this effect, cut out the desired shapes and place them on top of the base cookie before baking. You can even mix and match doughs. Dimensional cookies generally take no more time to bake than single-layer cookies.

SUGARING BEFORE BAKING OR ATTACHING CANDY ADD-ONS

Sugaring a cookie adds color and sparkle and couldn't be simpler: Just sprinkle the sugar on unbaked cookies, making sure to fully cover the areas you want to decorate. To attach other add-ons — candy, confetti, dragées, and so forth — press them firmly onto the unbaked cookies.

after-baking decorating techniques

A cookie decorated with royal icing is sure to impress — and even if your first tries are less than exquisite, the process is fun and creative. In this section you'll find royal icing recipes, a variety of techniques to use with the icing, and a wealth of information and tips to help you master the process. It might take a little practice to get the results you want, but you'll have a good time doing it.

Royal icing results are very weather dependent — you may get one result on a dry day, and find it much more challenging to achieve the same consistency when it's raining. Just remember, it all tastes good!

MAKING ROYAL ICING

Making royal icing is very easy, but it's not an exact science. Decorating success depends on the consistency of the icing, and there are many variables (especially weather), so read through the entire section carefully before you begin.

We provide three recipes that use three different forms of egg whites: powdered egg whites, liquid pasteurized egg whites, or meringue powder; we use them interchangeably, depending on what we have on hand. To make any of them, first ensure that your bowls are spotless. Any amount of grease will prevent the icing from whipping properly.

Lemon juice is our favorite royal icing flavoring, and vanilla extract is a good all-purpose flavoring, as well. You can experiment with other extracts too — for example, use peppermint in the icing for candy-cane cookies.

Although amounts will vary depending on your designs, in general a ½-pound recipe of piping royal icing and a 1-pound recipe of flood royal icing will pipe, flood, and detail two to three batches of rolled sugar cookies. Plan on more icing for elaborately iced cookies.

HANDY HINT

❋ ❋

While you're piping cookies, put a dampened paper towel or sponge at the bottom of a tall, heavy glass. When you're not using it, keep your pastry bag in the glass, tip-side down on the paper towel, to prevent the tip from becoming clogged. At the end of your session, place any unused royal icing in airtight containers and store in the refrigerator. Make sure to mix the icing well before using again.

ROYAL ICING RECIPES

ROYAL ICING USING POWDERED EGG WHITES	CONFECTIONERS' SUGAR	POWDERED EGG WHITES	WARM WATER*	LEMON JUICE OR VANILLA OR OTHER EXTRACT
FOR PIPING	2 cups (½ pound)	1 teaspoon	3 tablespoons	1 tablespoon (lemon juice) or ½–1 teaspoon (extract)
	4 cups (1 pound)	2 teaspoons	6 tablespoons	2 tablespoons (lemon juice) or 1–2 teaspoons (extract)
FOR FLOODING	2 cups (½ pound)	1 teaspoon	6 tablespoons	1 tablespoon (lemon juice) or ½–1 teaspoon (extract)
	4 cups (1 pound)	2 teaspoons	12 table-spoons	2 tablespoons (lemon juice) or 1–2 teaspoons (extract)

*Starting amount; you may need to add more, especially if you use an extract rather than lemon juice.

ROYAL ICING USING LIQUID PASTEURIZED EGG WHITES	CONFECTIONERS' SUGAR	LIQUID PASTEURIZED EGG WHITES	WARM WATER*	LEMON JUICE OR VANILLA OR OTHER EXTRACT
FOR PIPING	2 cups (½ pound)	3 tablespoons	1 tablespoon	1 tablespoon (lemon juice) or ½–1 teaspoon (extract)
	4 cups (1 pound)	6 tablespoons	2 tablespoons	2 tablespoons (lemon juice) or 1–2 teaspoons (extract)
FOR FLOODING	2 cups (½ pound)	3 tablespoons	3 tablespoons	1 tablespoon (lemon juice) or ½–1 teaspoon (extract)
	4 cups (1 pound)	6 tablespoons	6 tablespoons	2 tablespoons (lemon juice) or 1–2 teaspoons (extract)

*Starting amount; you may need to add more, especially if you use an extract rather than lemon juice.

ROYAL ICING USING MERINGUE POWDER	CONFECTIONERS' SUGAR	MERINGUE POWDER	WARM WATER*	LEMON JUICE OR VANILLA OR OTHER EXTRACT
FOR PIPING	2 cups (½ pound)	4 tablespoons	3 tablespoons	1 tablespoon (lemon juice) or ½–1 teaspoon (extract)
	4 cups (1 pound)	3 tablespoons	6 tablespoons	2 tablespoons (lemon juice) or 1–2 teaspoons (extract)
FOR FLOODING	2 cups (½ pound)	4 tablespoons	6 tablespoons	1 tablespoon (lemon juice) or ½–1 teaspoon (extract)
	4 cups (1 pound)	3 tablespoons	12 tablespoons	2 tablespoons (lemon juice) or 1–2 teaspoons (extract)

*Starting amount; you may need to add more, especially if you use an extract rather than lemon juice.

The method for making the icing is the same no matter what type of egg-white product you've used:

1 Combine all ingredients in the bowl of your electric mixer.

2 Beat on high for 5 minutes if you're using an electric stand mixer or for 10 minutes if you're using an electric hand mixer. (If your mixer has multiple attachments, use the paddle.)

3 When you reach the desired consistency, it's important that you immediately cover the mixture (it dries out quickly) or divide it into separate airtight containers for coloring (see page 19).

Use the water amounts in our icing recipes as starting points, but be prepared to adjust them depending on the weather or even your kitchen temperature. Be aware that the amount of water you add to the icing may change slightly every time you make it.

❊ PIPING CONSISTENCY TIPS

* When first mixed, piping icing will start out with the consistency of white glue. When you've finished beating the icing, it will be glossy, with a consistency similar to that of toothpaste.

Testing icing consistency

* The icing should squeeze easily out of a #2 tip but should stay in place and hold its shape on the cookie when it lands.

* If the icing is too stiff, it'll be hard to squeeze from the pastry bag and may lift up off the cookie when you finish the outline or detail.

* If the icing is too loose, it will spread and make too shallow an outline to dam the flood icing.

* Test the icing consistency before you fill the pastry bags. Just put a small amount into the tip and, pushing it through with your thumb, make a practice loop or two on a piece of waxed paper or your kitchen counter. Even though they might overlap, the loops should remain distinct rather than run together.

❊ FLOOD CONSISTENCY TIPS

* When first mixed, flood icing will appear very soupy. Never fear! In 5 minutes your icing will be shiny and white, with the consistency of heavy cream.

* This icing shouldn't be so thin that it runs like water or that its cookie coverage is transparent, and it shouldn't be so thick that it stays in place when you squirt it onto the cookie. It should immediately flow toward the piped borders.

* If your icing is too thick, add water 1 tablespoon at a time and beat for 1 minute after each addition. Test and repeat until you reach the desired consistency.

* If your icing is too thin, add confectioners' sugar 1 tablespoon at a time and beat for 1 minute after each addition. Test and repeat until you reach the desired consistency.

❋ COLORING YOUR ICING

1 To make each color icing, work with one airtight container at a time and keep the others tightly covered.

2 Add the desired food coloring, one drop at a time, to the icing (remember, you can always make a color deeper, but it's much harder to lighten it). Mix in the drops well until you have your desired color.

3 When matching flood and piping icing colors, you'll need to add different amounts of food coloring to each to achieve the same color because of the two icings' different consistencies.

❋ **PREPARING TO PIPE AND FLOOD.** This section explains how to set up pastry bags and fill squeeze bottles. You'll need one pastry bag set-up for each piping icing color and one squeeze bottle for each flood color.

Filling the Squeeze Bottle. After coloring your flood icing, pour each color into a separate squeeze bottle and screw on the top. If the squeeze top doesn't have a little cap, stick a toothpick in the hole to keep your icing from drying.

Filling the Pastry Bag

1 After you've colored your piping icing, hold a prepared pastry bag fitted with a #2 tip and cuff the bag over your fist. (See below.)

2 Using a spoon, scoop the icing into the bag as deep as you can toward the tip. Don't overfill the bag — half-full is ideal.

3 Unfold the bag and shake it firmly with a snapping motion so that the icing moves toward the tip. Twist the top of the bag to seal in the contents and compress the icing, minimizing any air pockets.

4 Fasten the bag with a twist tie at the top of the icing. Tightly tie a second twist tie toward the top end of the bag to seal in any icing smears on the upper part of the bag.

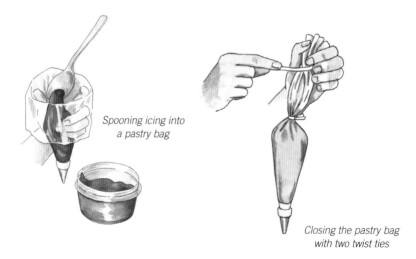

Spooning icing into a pastry bag

Closing the pastry bag with two twist ties

PUTTING THE TIP ON A PASTRY BAG

* *

1 *Unscrew the coupler and push the bigger threaded piece into the tip of the bag as far as it will go. (It should fit snugly; don't force it so far that you split the bag.)*

2 *Deeply score the bag with scissors just below the edge of the coupler. You now should be able to pull off the pastry bag tip about 2 inches from the end.*

3 *Place a metal pastry tip over the now-exposed opening of the threaded coupler piece and tightly screw the coupler ring over the tip and threads, catching the bag in the threads of the coupler in the process. If the coupler is on properly and tightly enough, the pastry tip will be stable.*

PIPING

Piping is the technique you will use most often, either to outline cookies to be flooded or to add embellishments. When piping, hold your pastry bag at a 45-degree angle above the surface of the cookie; you do not want to drag the tip. Use the heel of your palm to apply pressure to squeeze out the icing and the other hand to steady and guide the tip. If you're making dots, hold the bag straight up and down. Varying the pressure on the pastry bag will vary the thickness of the piping.

Holding and squeezing the pastry bag

✳ **OUTLINING.** Outlining a cookie creates a dam to hold the flood icing. Pipe around the cookie shape in an unbroken line, trying to get as close to the edge of the cookie as possible without falling off. When the outline reaches your starting point, lift the bag to end your line. If desired, use a toothpick to smooth out the connecting ends.

✱ **PIPING HEARTS.** Hearts are adorable and it takes just a minute to get the knack of making them. Simply pipe a short line for the left side of the heart, exerting a little more pressure at the start of the line and easing up at the end. Then make another line just like this for the right side of the heart, piping it to meet in a V with the first line.

✱ **PIPING GOOGLY EYES.** Pipe the following colors on top of one another in this order: white, an iris color (such as blue or brown), and black for the pupil. If you don't want the eyes to "pop," press on them lightly with a dampened finger to flatten. *Note: You can purchase ready-made icing eyes. See Resources.*

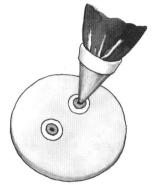

FLOODING

Once your cookie is outlined, it's ready to be filled, or flooded. Squeeze flood icing into the middle of the shape; it will flow toward the outline dam. Use a small offset spatula or a toothpick to coax the icing into the corners and up to the edges of the shape.

After being flooded, cookies have to dry undisturbed. Flood icing must dry for 2 to 3 hours before you can safely move cookies or add more layers of decorative detail without danger of smudging. Allow 24 hours before stacking, packing, or shipping flooded cookies.

Flooding a cookie

Filling all the corners

✻ **FLOODING ON WET FLOOD.** Squeezing contrasting flood icing on wet flood creates a painterly effect that's beautiful on many types of cookie designs. Try squeezing polka dots, stripes, or squiggles, or use a toothpick to create the feathered effects described on the following page. With flooding on wet flood, the colors will bleed into each other slightly, and may continue to bleed after drying.

Flooding straight lines on wet flood

* **FEATHERING STRIPES ON WET FLOOD.** Squeeze straight lines in a contrasting color of flood icing on wet flood. For a feathered effect, draw a toothpick perpendicularly through the stripes. For a "houndstooth" effect (such as on the wavy ornament on page 41), alternate toothpick direction with each row.

Creating feathered effect with a toothpick

* **FEATHERING DOTS (FOR HEARTS) AND SHORT LINES (FOR HOLLY) ON WET FLOOD.** Squeeze dots in a contrasting color of flood icing on wet flood. To create hearts, draw a toothpick through the middle of each dot. For a holly shape (such as on stocking cuff on page 137), flood short lines, and draw toothpick outward from center of line to create leaf points.

Feathering heart shapes

ADDING SUGAR SPARKLE

Sprinkle sanding sugar on wet piping or flood for color and sparkle, or use coconut for a snowy look. (See additional hint on page 95.) To add sparkle to a plain cookie background after baking, brush a little corn syrup on the cookie and sprinkle sugar on it.

ATTACHING CANDY ADD-ONS

Small candies or dragées stick readily to wet flood. Use tweezers if you want precise control over the placement. To attach add-ons to dry flood, use a dab of piping icing to affix.

WRITING WITH FOOD-SAFE MARKING PENS

These look just like Magic Markers and are especially good for decorating with small children, or to quickly write a name on a cookie to personalize it.

PAINTING WITH LUSTER DUST

To decorate cookies with luster or pearl dust, use a small, clean, dry paintbrush to scoop the dust into a small bowl. Mix it with a few drops of clear spirits, such as vodka or clear extracts (these evaporate and dry quickly), until the dust is dissolved into a thin liquid. Use the paintbrush to paint the mixture onto a plain cookie or onto dry royal icing for a decorative metallic or pearlized effect.

MAKING STAND-UP COOKIES

You can make your own easelbacks to create stand-up cookies. Taller cookies will need a half-rectangle easelback to support them; shorter cookies will stand up fine with a half-square. Cut squares or rectangles out of dough with a cutter (if you have one; use a paring knife if you don't). Cut the squares or rectangles in half diagonally with a paring knife. Either should be at least half the height of the cookie you wish to stand up. You'll need one triangle for each standing cookie. When your cookies are baked, decorated, and dry, affix a baked easelback to each one with piping icing. Stand up the cookie for a second or two before the icing dries to ensure that you've placed the easel-back for maximum steadiness, but dry the cookie face down (that is, easelback up). Once the icing glue is completely dry, the cookie will stand.

*Easelback attached
with icing*

cookie inspirations

STARRY, STARRY CHOCOLATE

From the Star of Bethlehem to the topper on your tree, stars are a wonderful symbol of Christmastime and a versatile shape to decorate.

Cookies and Icing
chocolate cookie dough
piping icing: red and white
flood icing: red

Equipment and Embellishments
large star cutter
smaller star cutter (to fit inside larger)
white nonpareils

Techniques
piping, flooding (pages 22, 24)
adding sugar sparkle (page 25)

1 Prepare, roll, and chill cookie dough according to recipe and rolling instructions.

2 Cut out equal numbers of star shapes in each of the two different sizes. Bake and cool according to recipe instructions.

3 Pipe and flood larger star cookie with red icing; allow to dry completely.

4 Pipe white outline ¼ inch from the edge of the smaller star; sprinkle with nonpareils while wet; allow to set. Gently shake off excess nonpareils.

5 Affix the smaller star to the larger star using a dot of piping icing as glue on the back of the smaller star, aligning star points. Pipe round dots on the larger star, around the edges of the smaller star.

PEPPERMINT GINGERBREAD HOUSE

Gingerbread has been a European holiday staple for centuries. Gingerbread houses became popular there and in America after the Brothers Grimm published their story "Hansel and Gretel."

Cookies and Icing
gingerbread cookie dough
piping icing: white

Equipment and Embellishments
house cutter
small rectangle cutter or paring
  knife
yellow hard candies, crushed
peppermint candies, crushed and
  whole
oblong silver dragées

Techniques
making windowpanes (page 13)
piping (page 22)
attaching candy add-ons
  (page 25)

1 Prepare, roll, and chill cookie dough according to recipe and rolling instructions.

2 Cut out house shapes. Cut out windows with a cookie cutter. Fill the windows with crushed yellow candies. Bake and cool according to windowpane instructions.

3 Pipe the roofline and chimney, filling in the chimney completely. While wet, sprinkle with crushed peppermint candy; allow to set. Gently shake off excess candy.

4 With piping icing, affix whole peppermint candies and pipe dot detail around candies. Pipe detail around windowpanes and on the gable peak. Affix dragées.

JOLLY HOLLY

Deck the halls — and the kitchen — with this colorful reminder of the holidays. This cookie version is easy and fun!

Cookies and Icing
green sugar cookie dough
piping icing: red

Equipment and Embellishments
holly leaf cutter

Techniques
coloring dough (page 13)
imprinting before baking
 (page 12)
piping (page 22)

1 Prepare, color, roll, and chill cookie dough according to recipe and coloring and rolling instructions.

2 Cut out holly leaf shapes. Imprint veins in the leaves with the back of a butter knife. Bake and cool according to recipe instructions.

3 Pipe red holly berries onto the end of each leaf.

COOKIE PLACE CARDS

Treat your guests to a personalized sweet with seasonally adorned cookie place cards. With an easelback, they can be made to stand up as shown here. Or, without an easelback, they can be set flat on your guests' plates.

Cookies and Icing
sugar cookie dough: uncolored and green (for embellishments)
piping icing: green, red, and white
flood icing: green and red

Equipment and Embellishments
rectangle and square cutters
small and mini cutters: snow-flake, star, candy cane
food-safe marking pen
round peppermint candy

Techniques
coloring dough (page 13)
piping, flooding (pages 22, 24)
attaching candy add-ons (page 25)
making stand-up cookies (page 26)
writing with food-safe marking pens (page 26)

1 Prepare, color, roll, and chill cookie dough according to recipe and rolling instructions.

2 Cut out rectangular place cards. Cut out squares to make easelbacks; cut squares in half diagonally with a paring knife. Cut out snowflake, star, and candy cane embellish-ments from uncolored or colored dough, as desired. Bake all shapes according to recipe instructions; cool completely.

3 Pipe and flood place cards; allow to dry com-pletely. Pipe designs on snowflakes; pipe stripes on candy cane.

4 When all icing is completely dry, write names on place cards using a food-safe marking pen. Affix embellishments to place-card cookies with piping icing. Pipe other designs, such as small snowflakes and dots.

5 Affix easelbacks to place cards with piping icing. Allow to dry.

✱ KEEP IT SIMPLE. Use colored dough to eliminate piping and flooding place card bases altogether.

CHEERY SNOWMAN

Make a batch of cheery, edible snowmen. They'll tide you over between snowfalls, until you can build the real thing!

Cookies and Icing
sugar cookie dough
piping icing: white, blue, and red
flood icing: white

Equipment and Embellishments
snowman cutter
black sanding sugar
green nonpareils
pretzel sticks

Techniques
piping, flooding (pages 22, 24)
adding sugar sparkle (page 25)
attaching candy add-ons
  (page 25)

1 Prepare, roll, and chill cookie dough according to recipe and rolling instructions.

2 Cut out snowman shapes. Bake and cool according to recipe instructions.

3 Pipe and flood entire snowman; allow to dry.

4 Pipe and flood second layer on hat area. While wet, carefully sprinkle black sanding sugar; allow to set. Gently shake off excess sugar.

5 Pipe buttons; sprinkle with green nonpareils; allow to set. Gently shake off excess nonpareils. Pipe eyes and mouth. Affix pretzel arms to back of cookie with icing.

MAN IN THE MOON SANTA

This cookie reminds us of folk art Santas. We think it's a fun interpretation — especially with a coconut pom-pom add-on!

Cookies and Icing
chocolate cookie dough
piping icing: white, flesh-tone, red, blue, black
flood icing: white, flesh-tone, red

Equipment and Embellishments
crescent moon cutter
small round cutter
flaked coconut
white sanding sugar

Techniques
piping, flooding (pages 22, 24)
adding sugar sparkle (page 25)
piping googly eyes (page 23)

1 Prepare, roll, and chill cookie dough according to recipe and rolling instructions.

2 Cut out moons; cut out the same number of circles for pom-poms. Bake and cool according to recipe instructions.

3 Pipe and flood red hat. Pipe and flood flesh-tone area of face. Pipe and flood beard. While wet, sprinkle beard with sanding sugar; allow to dry. Gently shake off excess sugar. Pipe and flood small round cookies. While wet, sprinkle with coconut; allow to dry. Gently shake off excess coconut.

4 Pipe decorative swirls on beard. While swirls are wet, sprinkle with sanding sugar; allow to set. Gently shake off excess. When beard is dry, pipe and flood mustache, then add lines and sanding sugar. Pipe and flood hatband to cover seam between face and red hat. Sprinkle with coconut.

5 Pipe googly eye. Pipe flesh-tone outline. Affix coconut pom-pom with piping icing.

* HANDY HINT. Round coconut
  cookies by themselves make
  great snowballs!

WAVY ORNAMENT

Round cookies are versatile — your ornament decorations are limited only by your imagination.

Cookies and Icing
gingerbread cookie dough
piping icing: light green, yellow, and blue
flood icing: light green and yellow

Equipment and Embellishments
round cutter
drinking straw
toothpicks
black licorice shoelace or ribbon

Techniques
making holes or cutouts (page 12)
piping, flooding (pages 22, 24)
feathering stripes on wet flood (page 25)

1 Prepare, roll, and chill cookie dough according to recipe and rolling instructions.

2 Cut out ornament circles; cut out a small hole in each circle with drinking straw. Bake and cool according to recipe instructions.

3 Pipe and flood entire cookie in green, working around hole. While wet, make three yellow stripes on green with yellow flood icing. Draw toothpick through flood stripes in alternate directions, per "houndstooth" feathering instructions. Allow to dry.

4 Pipe blue decorative dots as shown; pipe decorative yellow stripes around the poles. Add licorice or ribbon to hang ornament.

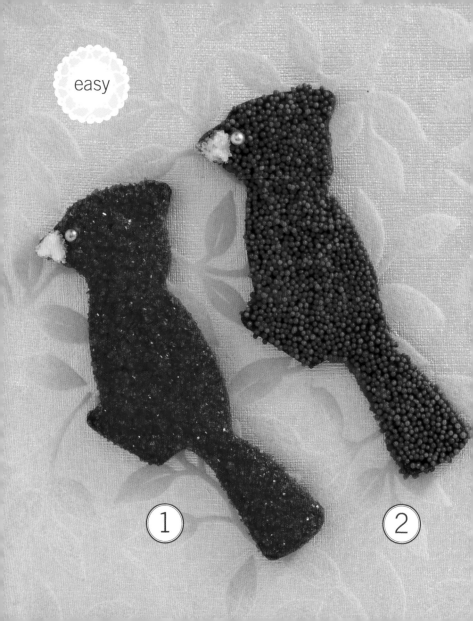

easy

1

2

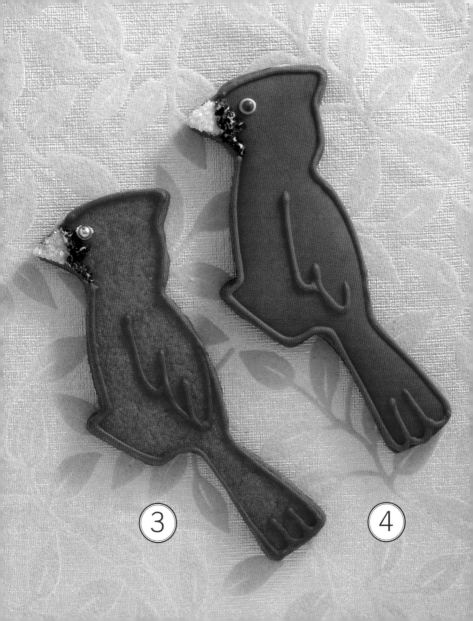

COLORFUL CARDINALS

**Red cardinals on green branches remind us of the colors of Christmas.
On a snowy day, their natural beauty never fails to take our breath away.
Variations #1 and #2 are embellished before baking; #3 and #4 use
after-baking techniques.**

CARDINALS #1 AND #2

Cookies and Icing
cookie dough of your choice

Equipment and Embellishments
cardinal cutter
sanding sugar: yellow and red
red nonpareils
dragées

Techniques
sugaring before baking (page 13)
attaching candy add-ons
  (page 13)

1 Prepare, roll, and chill cookie dough according to recipe and rolling instructions.

2 Cut out cardinal shapes. Sprinkle with sanding sugar (cookie #1) or red nonpareils (cookie #2), avoiding the beak area. Sprinkle beak area with yellow sanding sugar. Press in dragée eye.

3 Bake and cool according to recipe instructions.

Cookies and Icing

cookie dough of your choice (for
  cookie #4) or red sugar cookie
  dough (for cookie #3)
piping icing: red, white, and blue
flood icing: red

Equipment and Embellishments

cardinal cutter
sanding sugar: yellow and black

Techniques

coloring dough (page 13)
piping, flooding (pages 22, 24)
adding sugar sparkle (page 25)
piping googly eyes (page 23)

1 Prepare cookie dough according to recipe.
   For cookie #3, color dough red. Roll, and chill
   according to rolling instructions.

2 Cut out cardinal shapes. Bake and cool
   according to recipe instructions.

3 For cookie #3, pipe facial markings (black
   area) with white piping icing; sprinkle with
   black sanding sugar. Allow to set and gently
   shake off excess sugar. Pipe beak area; sprinkle with yellow sanding sugar. Allow to set and
   gently shake off excess sugar. Pipe bird outline
   and wing and tail detail. Affix dragée eye with
   piping icing.

4 For cookie #4, pipe and flood entire cookie
   in red; allow to dry completely. Pipe facial
   markings (black area) with white piping icing;
   sprinkle with black sanding sugar. Allow to set
   and gently shake off excess sugar. Pipe beak
   area; sprinkle with yellow sanding sugar. Allow
   to set and gently shake off excess sugar. Pipe
   bird outline and wing and tail detail. Pipe googly eye according to instructions.

FANCIFUL SLEIGH PARTY FAVOR

These cookie "boxes" are perfect for holding small Christmas treats and can double as holiday table decorations.

Cookies and Icing
chocolate cookie dough
piping icing: red

Equipment and Embellishments
sleigh cutter
1½-inch square cutter
gold luster dust
clear spirits
small paintbrush
gold dragées

Techniques
painting with luster dust
  (page 26)
piping (page 22)
making cookie boxes (see
  following page)

1 Read "Making Cookie Boxes" instructions on the following page before you begin. Prepare, roll, and chill cookie dough according to recipe and rolling instructions.

2 Cut out sleigh, reverse sleigh, and three box squares for each box. Bake and cool according to recipe instructions.

3 Paint luster dust on outsides of sleigh and reverse sleighs. Allow to dry.

4 Pipe decorative red design. Affix dragées on sleigh runners with piping icing. Allow to dry.

5 Assemble boxes, per instructions. When sleighs and boxes are completely dry, assemble per instructions. Fill with desired goodies.

MAKING COOKIE BOXES

For each cookie box (see the sleigh on page 46), you'll need three squares — for the box bottom, front, and back — and two cutter shapes for the sides (be sure to bake the side shapes as mirror opposites). After you have baked and cooled the cookies, decorate the sides — again, as mirror opposites so that each of the left- and right-decorated sides will face outward — and allow them to dry. While the decorated cookies are drying, use royal icing to glue together the box frames. Let them dry completely; you can use your cookie slats to support the frames while they dry. Finally, glue two decorated sides to each cookie frame, let the creations dry overnight, then fill with candy or other treats.

Letting the cookie box frame dry

DOUBLE-SIDED COOKIE POPS

Cookie pops (see pops on page 50) require two cookies so that the pops will have two decorated sides. To make each pop, cut out two cookies of the same shape (if you use a shape other than round, be sure to bake mirror opposites) and place a lollipop stick under one of them, pressing down gently to embed the stick. (If you're making 12 pops, you'll attach sticks to 12 of your 24 cookies.) Bake the cookies as directed. After the cookies have cooled, decorate the top of each cookie as desired. When they're completely dry, use royal icing to glue together the two cookies back to back.

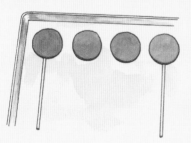

Sticks attached to half the cookies

Gluing cookies together

These festive, double-sided cookie pops evoke old-fashioned candies. Flavors like peppermint and chocolate are classic holiday combination.

Cookies and Icing

cookie dough of your choice
piping icing: dark red, light red,
    dark green, and light green
flood icing: dark red, light red,
    dark green, and light green

Equipment and Embellishments

round cutter
lollipop sticks

Techniques

double-sided cookie pops (see
    previous page)
piping, flooding (pages 22, 24)
flooding on wet flood (page 24)

1 Read "Double-sided Cookie Pops" instructions on the previous page before you begin. Prepare, roll, and chill cookie dough according to recipe and rolling instructions.

2 Cut out round cookies. Embed lollipop sticks before baking, per instructions. Bake and cool according to recipe instructions.

3 Pipe and flood all cookies: one color for each cookie. While wet, use flood icing in a contrasting color to create swirl pattern. Allow to dry completely.

4 Assemble lollipops, per directions.

✳ **KEEP IT SIMPLE:** Pipe and flood cookies with white vanilla or peppermint icing; while wet, sprinkle on crushed peppermint candy. Allow to dry; gently shake off excess candy.

EASY, ELEGANT WREATHS

These welcoming evergreen symbols adorn neighborhood doors and shop windows — now they can enliven your cookie plate!

Cookies and Icing
green sugar cookie dough
piping icing: red

Equipment and Embellishments
round, fluted cutter
smaller round, fluted cutter
paring knife

Techniques
coloring dough (page 13)
imprinting before baking
  (page 12)
piping (page 22)

1 Prepare green dough; roll and chill according to recipe and rolling instructions.

2 Cut out wreaths and wreath centers. Imprint leaf designs on cookie with the tip of a paring knife, as shown on cookie #1, if desired. Bake and cool according to recipe instructions.

3 Pipe red berries in clusters.

✳ **KEEP IT SIMPLE.** Instead of using royal icing, sprinkle on a few red nonpareils before baking for even easier "berries."

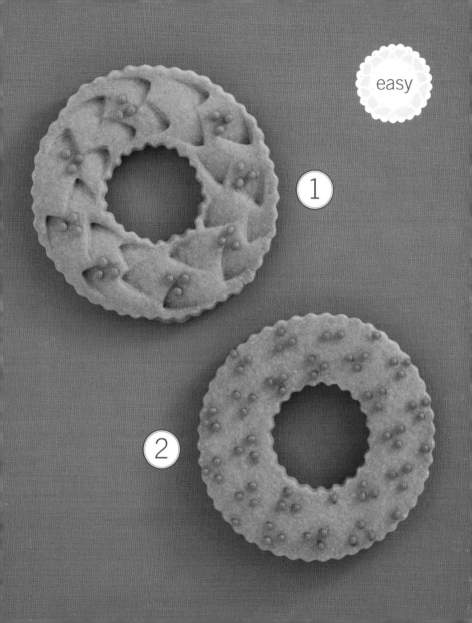

SNOWY CHRISTMAS TREE

Use your imagination to create an unexpected holiday palette — here's a departure from the usual green tree.

Cookies and Icing
gingerbread cookie dough
piping icing: white, light blue,
  red, and light green
flood icing: white

*Equipment and
Embellishments*
tree cutter
gold luster dust
clear spirits
small paintbrush

Techniques
piping, flooding (pages 22, 24)
painting with luster dust
  (page 26)

1 Prepare, roll, and chill cookie dough according to recipe and rolling instructions.

2 Cut out tree shapes. Bake and cool according to recipe instructions.

3 Pipe and flood white tree body, leaving trunk bare. Allow to dry completely.

4 Paint garland with gold luster dust; allow to dry completely.

5 Pipe light blue dots; pipe red dots. While red dots are still wet, pipe green dots on top.

COZY WINTER WARMERS

When the winter winds howl, pull out your fashionable hats and mittens. Or stay in to bake, decorate, and eat them!

Cookies and Icing
cookie dough of your choice
piping icing: red and green
flood icing: red and green

Equipment and Embellishments
mitten cutter
winter hat cutter
sanding sugar: red and green

Techniques
piping, flooding (pages 22, 24)
flooding on wet flood (page 24)
adding sugar sparkle (page 25)

1 Prepare, roll, and chill cookie dough according to recipe and rolling instructions.

2 Cut out mittens and hats. Bake and cool according to recipe instructions.

3 Pipe and flood entire hat cookie with red icing; while wet, use flood icing to create green stripes. Pipe and flood entire mitten cookie with green icing. While wet, use flood icing to create red stripes. Allow to dry completely.

4 Pipe and flood hatband and pom-pom on hat with green icing. While wet, sprinkle with green sanding sugar. When set, gently shake off excess sugar. Pipe and flood mitten wristband with red icing. While wet, sprinkle with red sanding sugar. When set, gently shake off excess sugar.

Kids know that when the lights go up, Christmas is just around the corner. These cookie versions can be strung up like the real ones!

Cookies and Icing
cookie dough of your choice
piping icing: white
flood icing: white

Equipment and Embellishments
Christmas lightbulb cutter
drinking straw
silver luster dust
clear spirits
small paintbrush
sanding sugar: green, red, yellow, and white
licorice shoelace

Techniques
making holes or cutouts (page 12)
piping, flooding (pages 22, 24)
adding sugar sparkle (page 25)
painting with luster dust (page 26)

1 Prepare, roll, and chill cookie dough according to recipe and rolling instructions.

2 Cut out lightbulbs. Cut out a small hole in each bulb with a drinking straw. Bake and cool according to recipe instructions.

3 Pipe "thread" lines on the ends of bulbs. Pipe and flood main part of bulb. While flood icing is wet, carefully sugar main part of bulb, being careful not to get sugar on "thread" lines. Allow to dry completely; gently shake off excess sugar.

4 Paint end of bulb with silver luster dust. Allow to dry.

5 String bulbs with licorice shoelace. If hanging, knot the lace at each cookie so they stay in place.

SWEET SEASON'S GREETINGS

Forget e-cards — hand-deliver these thoughtful "notes" to friends and neighbors. They're truly a special delivery.

Cookies and Icing
cookie dough of your choice
piping icing: red and green
flood icing: red

Equipment and Embellishments
rectangle cutter or paring knife
food-safe marking pen
pink mini dragées
flat dragées
silver Jordan almonds

Techniques
piping, flooding (pages 22, 24)
writing with food-safe marking
  pens (page 26)
attaching candy add-ons
  (page 25)

1 Prepare, roll, and chill cookie dough according to recipe and rolling instructions.

2 Cut out rectangles, or use a knife to cut cards freehand. Bake and cool according to recipe instructions.

3 Pipe and flood entire cookie red; allow to dry completely.

4 Write message with food-safe marking pen. Pipe holly leaves and decorative green detail; allow to set.

5 Affix holly berry dragées and silver embellishments.

Happy
Holidays
from the
Morrison family

TRADITIONAL PERNICKY DOVE

These designs are traditional for Eastern European versions of gingerbread, called *pernicky* in Czechoslovakia and *piernik* in Poland. These folksy, lacy designs look intricate, but since they require only basic piping, they're relatively easy to do.

Cookies and Icing
gingerbread cookie dough
piping icing: white

Equipment and Embellishments
dove cutter

Techniques
piping (page 22)

1 Prepare, roll, and chill cookie dough according to recipe and rolling instructions.

2 Cut out dove shapes; bake and cool according to recipe instructions.

3 Pipe designs; allow to dry completely.

easy

THE STAR OF THE TABLE

Here's a three-dimensional cookie project to grace a holiday table or buffet sideboard.

Cookies and Icing
gingerbread cookie dough
piping icing: white
confectioners' sugar

Equipment and Embellishments
set of five graduated star cutters
(ours range from 2½ to
6½ inches)
multicolored dragées

Techniques
attaching candy add-ons
(page 25)

1 Prepare, roll, and chill cookie dough according to recipe and rolling instructions.

2 Cut out three sets of stars, plus one extra of the smallest (16 cookies total). Bake and cool according to recipe instructions. Affix dragées to the points of each star with piping icing; allow to dry completely.

3 Lightly sprinkle confectioners' sugar on one of the largest stars. Pipe icing onto center back and glue a second star of the same size to the top of the first star, alternating points. Sprinkle sugar on top star.

4 Continue gluing stars together, from larger stars to smaller, alternating points and sprinkling sugar on each layer. Leave smallest star for top.

5 When tree is assembled, affix top star in an upright position by piping a generous amount of icing to two bottom points. (You may need to prop it with crumpled aluminum foil until it's dry.)

O TANNENBAUM

A paring knife gives easy, elegant detail to a gingerbread tree.

Cookies and Icing
gingerbread cookie dough
piping icing: red, blue, light
  green, and white

*Equipment and
Embellishments*
tree cutter
paring knife
white sanding sugar
dragées

Techniques
imprinting before baking
  (page 12)
piping (page 22)
adding sugar sparkle (page 25)

1 Prepare, roll, and chill cookie dough according to recipe and rolling instructions.

2 Cut out tree shapes. Imprint dimensional details with the point of a paring knife. Bake and cool according to recipe instructions.

3 Pipe colored dots for ornaments, and affix dragée at top of tree. While wet, sprinkle ornaments with sanding sugar. When dry, shake off excess sugar.

✳ **KEEP IT SIMPLE.** To eliminate piping icing, lightly press dragées or other sugar decorations onto tree after imprinting design, but before baking.

BLADES OF GLORY

For munching during skating parties or while watching triple axels from the couch, ice skates always mean winter fun.

Cookies and Icing
gingerbread cookie dough
piping icing: white and blue
flood icing: white

Equipment and Embellishments
ice skate cutter
silver luster dust
clear spirits
small paintbrush
white sanding sugar

Techniques
piping, flooding (pages 22, 24)
painting with luster dust
  (page 26)
adding sugar sparkle (page 25)

1 Prepare, roll, and chill cookie dough according to recipe and rolling instructions.

2 Cut out skates. Bake and cool according to recipe instructions.

3 Pipe and flood boot of skate; allow to dry.

4 Paint blade with luster dust; allow to dry.

5 Pipe laces; allow to dry. Pipe pom-poms; while wet, sprinkle with sanding sugar. When dry, gently shake off excess sugar.

EASY SNOWFLAKES

It's quick to make a blizzard's worth of these easy flurries, so they're great to bring to parties or holiday bake sales.

Cookies and Icing
gingerbread or chocolate cookie
  dough
piping icing: white

*Equipment and
Embellishments*
round cutter

Techniques
piping (page 22)

1 Prepare, roll, and chill cookie dough according to recipe and rolling instructions.

2 Cut out round cookies. Bake and cool according to recipe instructions.

3 Pipe snowflake designs on cookies; allow to dry completely.

easy

PARTRIDGES AND A PEAR

Translate one of the season's most beloved carols into lyrical cookie creations.

....

PARTRIDGES

Cookies and Icing
sugar cookie dough
piping icing: light brown, white,
   yellow, and green
flood icing: light brown, white,
   and red

Equipment and Embellishments
partridge cutter
toothpicks

Techniques
piping, flooding (pages 22, 24)
feathering stripes on wet flood
   (page 25)
piping googly eyes (page 23)

1   Prepare, roll, and chill cookie dough according to recipe and rolling instructions.

2   Cut out partridges. Bake and cool according to recipe instructions.

3   Pipe and flood entire cookie with brown icing. While wet, make white stripes with flood icing on tail and back. Drag toothpick through stripes in tail to head direction. Make parallel, adjacent stripes in red and white flood on chest and neck of bird. Drag clean toothpick through stripes in tail to head direction. Make red dot on tip of head plumage; drag clean toothpick through end of plumage. Allow to dry completely.

4   Pipe eye and beak. Allow to dry.

Cookies and Icing
sugar cookie dough
piping icing: light green and red
flood icing: light green

Equipment and Embellishments
pear cutter
white sanding sugar

Techniques
piping, flooding (pages 22, 24)
adding sugar sparkle (page 25)

1   Prepare, roll, and chill cookie dough according to recipe and rolling instructions.

2   Cut out pears. Bake and cool according to recipe instructions.

3   Pipe and flood entire pear in light green. Allow to dry completely.

4   Pipe lattice pattern in light green; while wet, sprinkle with sanding sugar. Allow to dry; gently shake off excess sugar.

5   Pipe red dots at intersections of lines; pipe stem. Allow to dry.

This cookie reminds us of the trees we see while on the road, in the backs of trucks or lashed to the roofs of cars, on their way to brighten homes with evergreen cheer.

Cookies and Icing

chocolate cookie dough
piping icing: red, green, and white
flood icing: red

Equipment and Embellishments

truck with tree cutter
flaked coconut or white sanding
  sugar
flat dragées or flat, round candy-
  coated chocolates

Techniques

piping, flooding (pages 22, 24)
attaching candy add-ons
  (page 25)
adding sugar sparkle (page 25)

1 Prepare, roll, and chill cookie dough according to recipe and rolling instructions.

2 Cut out truck shapes. Bake and cool according to recipe instructions.

3 Pipe and flood body of truck. Allow to dry.

4 Pipe truck and wheel detail in red. Pipe tree design in green. Affix hubcap dragées with piping icing.

5 When set, pipe headlight. Sprinkle with coconut or sugar; allow to dry. Gently shake off excess.

PRETTY POINSETTIAS

The botanical name for this lovely plant means "very beautiful." Native to Mexico and brought to the United States in the 1820s, today the poinsettia is practically synonymous with Christmas.

Cookies and Icing
chocolate cookie dough
piping icing: light red
flood icing: light red and dark red

Equipment and Embellishments
poinsettia cutter
toothpicks
gold dragées

Techniques
piping, flooding (pages 22, 24)
feathering short lines on wet flood
  (page 25)
attaching candy add-ons
  (page 25)

1 Prepare, roll, and chill dough according to recipe and rolling instructions.

2 Cut out poinsettias. Bake and cool according to recipe instructions.

3 For cookie #1, pipe and flood light red icing. While wet, draw leaf veins from the center of the plant to the tips of the bract (leaf). Drag a toothpick outward from center of vein lines towards edges of bract. Allow to dry.

4 For cookie #2, pipe with light red and flood with dark red icing; allow to dry completely.

5 For either variation, pipe outlines and detail of bracts. Use piping icing to affix dragées to center.

WINTER WONDERLAND SNOWGLOBE

These fanciful novelties bring a bit of the snowy weather indoors. Ours can be made with a round cutter. It won't sit around long enough to collect any dust!

Cookies and Icing
chocolate cookie dough
piping icing: green, white, and
  light brown
flood icing: green, red, and white

Equipment and Embellishments
round cutter
dragées
corn syrup
pastry brush
white nonpareils

Techniques
piping, flooding (pages 22, 24)
flooding on wet flood (page 24)
adding sugar sparkle (page 25)

1 Prepare, roll, and chill cookie dough according to recipe and rolling instructions.

2 Cut out round cookies. Bake and cool according to recipe instructions.

3 Pipe and flood green tree shape; while wet, dot with red flood. Pipe light brown tree trunk. Allow to dry.

4 Pipe and flood snowy base. Lightly brush bare cookie with corn syrup, then pipe snowy trim on tree. While base, corn syrup, and trim are wet, sprinkle nonpareils on all. Allow to dry; gently shake to remove excess.

5 Affix dragée tree topper with piping icing

PEACE DOVES

Peace on Earth. We can't think of a more wonderful sentiment, and this universal symbol says it tastefully.

Cookies and Icing
sugar cookie dough: uncolored and green
piping icing: green

Equipment and Embellishments
dove cutter
oval "leaf" shape cutter (from aspic cutter set)

Techniques
adding dimension to cookies (page 13)
piping (page 22)

1 Prepare, roll, and chill cookie doughs according to recipe and rolling instructions.

2 Cut out doves from sugar cookie dough; cut out leaves (3 to 5 for each dove) from green dough. Place green leaves on doves. Bake and cool according to recipe instructions.

3 Pipe stems of olive branch.

✳ **KEEP IT SIMPLE.** Omit the piped stems for a super-simple cookie.

CRAZY CANDY CANES

Lore has it that candy "canes" were first given to children to ensure their good behavior in church. Whether it's true or not, these quintessential holiday confections never fail to bring out the kid in each of us!

Cookies and Icing
chocolate cookie dough
piping icing in base color
flood icing in base color and
   contrasting color

*Equipment and
Embellishments*
candy cane cutter
toothpicks

Techniques
piping, flooding (pages 22, 24)
feathering stripes on wet flood
   (page 25)

1   Prepare, roll, and chill cookie dough according to recipe and rolling instructions.

2   Cut out candy cane shapes. Bake and cool according to recipe instructions.

3   Pipe and flood with base color. While wet, create three parallel stripes in contrasting color, following contours of candy cane from the top of the crook to the bottom of the cane.

4   Drag toothpick through wet flood across candy cane; repeat, in same direction along entire length of cane. Allow to dry.

CHOO-CHOO STEAM ENGINE

Once a favorite toy to discover under the Christmas tree, train sets have come to be an enduring icon of the season.

Cookies and Icing
sugar cookie dough
piping icing: red and white
flood icing: red

Equipment and Embellishments
train engine cutter
luster dust: silver and gold
clear spirits
small paintbrush
flat silver dragées

Techniques
piping, flooding (pages 22, 24)
painting with luster dust
  (page 26)
attaching candy add-ons
  (page 25)

1 Prepare, roll, and chill cookie dough according to recipe and rolling instructions.

2 Cut out train engines. Bake and cool according to recipe instructions.

3 Pipe train body and front details; flood main portion of train body. Allow to dry. Paint gold luster details on smokestack and front of train engine; allow to dry.

4 Pipe cow-catcher and wheel details in white. Pipe outline of entire train and details in red. Pipe rod connecting the two wheels. Affix silver dragées with piping icing.

5 When piping icing is dry, paint silver luster dust on cow-catcher and rod that connects the wheels.

MARCHING TOY SOLDIER

Straight from a scene in the Nutcracker ballet, this detailed toy soldier will require some extra effort, but he won't fail to impress!

Cookies and Icing
gingerbread cookie dough
piping icing: green, flesh-tone, red, and blue
flood icing: green, flesh-tone, red, and blue

Equipment and Embellishments
marching soldier cutter
gold luster dust
clear spirits
small paintbrush
dragées: gold and elongated silver
black sanding sugar

Techniques
piping, flooding (pages 22, 24)
adding sugar sparkle (page 25)
painting with luster dust (page 26)

1 Prepare, roll, and chill cookie dough according to recipe and rolling instructions.

2 Cut out soldiers. Bake and cool according to recipe instructions.

3 Pipe and flood hat, jacket, and trousers in that order. Pipe and flood hands; pipe and flood face last. Pipe outline of trumpet with flesh-colored piping.

4 While red flood is wet, place dragée buttons on jacket. While face is wet, use a snack-size ziplock bag with small corner cut out to sprinkle black sanding sugar for soldier's hair. Allow all icing to dry completely.

5 Pipe outline and stripe detail on trousers; pipe eye. Pipe outline and details on jacket; pipe red cheek. Pipe outline on face and hand. Pipe outline on hat and affix elongated dragée. Paint luster dust on horn, trouser stripe, and jacket details. Allow to dry completely.

CRACKLING CANDY FIREPLACE

Santa might have to use the door if the fire's roaring — but leave him an imaginative cookie treat and he won't hold it against you.

Cookies and Icing
gingerbread cookie dough
piping icing: white, red, and green
flood icing: white and red

Equipment and Embellishments
rectangle cutter
paring knife
red or orange hard candies, crushed
chocolate bar

Techniques
making windowpanes (page 13)
piping, flooding (pages 22, 24)
flooding over dry piping (see facing page)
attaching candy add-ons (page 25)

1 Prepare, roll, and chill cookie dough according to recipe and rolling instructions.

2 Cut out rectangles. Cut out flame shapes with paring knife. Fill flames with crushed red candy. Bake and cool according to recipe instructions.

3 Pipe bricks in grid pattern around flame of fireplace; allow to set. Flood over piped grid. Allow to dry.

4 Pipe and flood stockings; pipe green details on wet flood.

5 Chop chocolate bar into shards for logs (you may substitute pretzel sticks). Affix under candy flame with red piping icing. Dot additional "embers" around logs with red piping icing. Allow to dry.

✳ **FLOODING OVER DRY PIPING.** Pipe the cookie outline and the desired detail (here, it's bricks). When the piping icing is dry to the touch, flood the entire shape, letting the flood icing flow over the piped lines.

ELEGANT, EASY CHRISTMAS TREE

You can make a forest's worth of these trees in no time — the green dough and imprinting makes them simple and pretty.

Cookies and Icing
green sugar cookie dough
piping icing: white
flood icing: white

Equipment and Embellishments
tree cutter
paring knife
gold luster dust
clear spirits
small paintbrush

Techniques
imprinting before baking
  (page 12)
piping, flooding (pages 22, 24)
painting with luster dust
  (page 26)

1 Prepare, roll, and chill cookie dough according to recipe and rolling instructions.

2 Cut out tree shapes. Imprint branch designs with the tip of a paring knife. Bake and cool according to recipe instructions.

3 Pipe and flood star; allow to dry.

4 Paint star with luster dust; allow to dry.

∗ **ICING DECORATIONS.** Use leftover icing to make simple, fun shapes (stars, hearts, eyeballs, leaves) on parchment or waxed paper. Let them dry completely and store carefully in an airtight container. Peel them off to use when you want to make superfast, simple cookies!

easy

SANTA'S ADORABLE ELVES

Make a whole workshop full of Santa's helpers — their outfits can be as lively and individual as your imagination allows!

Cookies and Icing

cookie dough of your choice

piping icing: red, dark green, light green, white

flood icing: red, dark green, light green

Equipment and Embellishments

gnome/elf cutter

toothpicks

sanding sugar: white and black

dragées

Techniques

piping, flooding (pages 22, 24)

flooding on wet flood (page 24)

adding sugar sparkle (page 25)

1 Prepare, roll, and chill cookie dough according to recipe and rolling instructions.

2 Cut out elf shapes. Bake and cool according to recipe instructions.

3 Pipe and flood hats and outfits in desired colors. While flood is wet, add polka dots. For collar detail (on #2), flood small dots on wet flood in contrasting color. Pull points out from dots with a toothpick.

4 For sugared hat bands, pom-poms, and collar (on #2): Pipe white dots around collar and/or hatband, and on tip of hat. Sprinkle with white sanding sugar (or leave plain); allow to set. Gently tap off excess sugar.

5 For sugared boots (on #1): Pipe and flood boots. Sprinkle with black sanding sugar; allow to set. Gently tap off excess sugar.

6 Pipe clothing outlines, belts, face details, nonsugared hatbands and pom-poms. Affix dragées on belts. Allow to dry completely.

* **PERFECT POURING TECHNIQUE.** To better direct the flow of your sanding, fill a snack-size ziplock bag with the sugar, snip off a small corner of the bag, and sprinkle with precision.

SNOW-DUSTED PINECONE

A walk through the wintery forest yields an armful of simple and natural decorations. We like the real ones piled in pretty bowls — and these piled on our cookie plates.

Cookies and Icing
gingerbread cookie dough
confectioners' sugar

Equipment and Embellishments
pinecone cutter
paring knife

Techniques
imprinting before baking
  (page 12)

1 Prepare, roll, and chill cookie dough according to recipe and rolling instructions.

2 Cut out pinecones. Imprint textured design with the tip of a paring knife. Bake and cool according to recipe instructions.

3 Sprinkle with confectioners' sugar, shaking cookie to make sugar pool in crevices.

easy

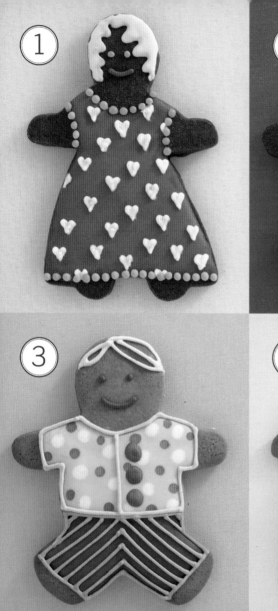

CHEERY COOKIE PEOPLE

Give your traditional gingerbread men and women a fun fashion personality! Or make them in chocolate, for a new twist on old favorite shapes. Use your favorite color combinations — we list the icing colors for all the "outfits" pictured here.

Cookies and Icing

gingerbread or chocolate cookie dough

piping icing: red, dark blue, light blue, tan, light green, white, light yellow

flood icing: red, dark blue, light blue, tan, light green, white, light yellow

Equipment and Embellishments

gingerbread man and gingerbread woman cutters

toothpicks

white nonpareils

Techniques

piping, flooding (pages 22, 24)

flooding on wet flood (page 24)

feathering dots (for hearts) on wet flood (page 25)

feathering stripes on wet flood (page 25)

piping hearts (page 23)

adding sugar sparkle (page 25)

1 Prepare, roll, and chill cookie dough according to recipe and rolling instructions.

2 Cut out men and women. Bake and cool according to recipe instructions.

3 Create individual outfits as follows:

Cookie #1: Pipe and flood dress; allow to dry. Pipe hearts on dress; pipe green dots on neckline, sleeves, and hemline. Pipe face and hair.

Cookie #2: Pipe and flood trousers; pipe and flood shirt. While shirt is wet, make two lines of dots with red flood; draw toothpick through dots in opposite directions to make hearts. Allow to dry. Pipe trouser and shirt outlines; pipe collar detail and buttons. Pipe face and hair.

Cookie #3: Pipe and flood trousers; pipe and flood shirt. While shirt is wet, make polka dots with wet flood. Allow to dry. Pipe outline and stripes on trousers; pipe outline and detail on shirt. Pipe buttons. Pipe face and hair.

Cookie #4: Pipe and flood dress. While wet, make parallel stripes across cookie with wet flood; draw toothpick through (perpendicular to stripes), alternating up and down direction. Allow to dry. Pipe and flood apron in white. While flood is wet, make dots with wet flood. Allow to dry. Pipe apron detail. Pipe face and hair.

Cookie #5: Pipe and flood trousers; pipe and flood shirt. While shirt is wet, make dots with red flood; dot green flood in the centers of red dots. Allow to dry. Pipe outline and detail on trousers and shirt; pipe buttons. Pipe face and hair.

Cookie #6: Pipe and flood dress. Allow to dry. Pipe sash and stripes along hem. While wet, sprinkle with nonpareils; allow to dry. Gently shake off excess nonpareils. Pipe polka dot details on skirt and dots on sleeve and neckline. Pipe face and hair.

Cookie #7: Pipe and flood dress. While wet, make lines of dots with red flood along neckline and hemline. Draw toothpick through dots to make hearts. Allow to dry. Pipe belt; pipe face and hair.

Cookie #8: Pipe and flood trousers; pipe and flood shirt in red. While shirt icing is wet, flood yellow stripes on wet flood. Allow to dry. Pipe outlines and details on shirt and trousers. Pipe face and hair.

CHRISTMAS BELLS ARE RINGING!

Some of our favorite carols feature bells — "Hark, How the Bells!," "Silver Bells," and, of course, "Jingle Bells." Although they don't make a sound, tasters will give these bells a ringing endorsement!

Cookies and Icing
gingerbread cookie dough
piping icing: light blue, light
  green, and red

*Equipment and
Embellishments*
bell cutter
trefoil shape cutter (from aspic
  cutter set)
drinking straw

Techniques
making holes or cutouts (page 12)
piping (page 22)
piping hearts (page 23)

1 Prepare, roll, and chill cookie dough according to recipe and rolling instructions.

2 Cut out bells; cut holes in dough with trefoil aspic cutter or drinking straw. Bake and cool according to recipe instructions.

3 Pipe stripes, dots, and heart detail.

easy

INTERPRETIVE SNOWFLAKE

This snowflake borrows its design from the Czech and Polish gingerbread traditions. Fanciful and lovely, it uses just one color of piping icing.

Cookies and Icing
gingerbread cookie dough
piping icing: white

Equipment and Embellishments
snowflake cutter

Techniques
piping (page 22)

1 Prepare, roll, and chill cookie dough according to recipe and rolling instructions.

2 Cut out snowflakes. Bake and cool according to recipe instructions.

3 Pipe lacy design; allow to dry.

easy

OLD-FASHIONED ORNAMENTS

Gold-burnished with luster dust, these cookies remind us of the precious — and breakable! — tree decorations of old.

Cookies and Icing

sugar cookie dough

piping icing: light blue, dark blue, dark red, light red, light green, light blue

flood icing: light blue, dark red, light green

Equipment and Embellishments

ornament cutters

gold luster dust

clear spirits

small paintbrush

Techniques

piping, flooding (pages 22, 24)

painting with luster dust (page 26)

1 Prepare, roll, and chill cookie dough according to recipe and rolling instructions.

2 Cut out ornaments. Bake and cool according to recipe instructions.

3 Pipe and flood in desired color; allow to dry.

4 Paint stripes on dry icing with luster dust; allow to dry.

5 Pipe contrasting stripes and dots over luster dust.

CHRISTMAS DELIVERY SLEIGH

Who doesn't listen for hoofbeats on the roof on Christmas Eve? With the help of licorice shoelaces, Santa's team pulls a sleigh-full of gifts to delight the recipient!

SLEIGH

Cookies and Icing
gingerbread cookie dough
piping icing: red, white, light
  green, dark green, light blue
flood icing: red, light green, light
  blue

*Equipment and
Embellishments*
sleigh cutter
white sanding sugar
luster dust
clear spirits
small paintbrush

Techniques
piping, flooding (pages 22, 24)
adding sugar sparkle (page 25)
painting with luster dust
  (page 26)

1 Prepare, roll, and chill cookie dough according to recipe and rolling instructions.

2 Cut out sleighs. Bake and cool according to recipe instructions.

3 Pipe and flood body of sleigh. Pipe and flood gift boxes. Allow to dry.

4 Pipe and flood outline of sleigh and polka dots in red. Pipe snowy trim in white. Sprinkle outline, dots, and trim with white sanding sugar. Allow to dry. Gently shake off excess sugar.

5 Pipe ribbons on gift boxes; pipe sleigh runner. When runner is dry, paint with gold luster dust.

Cookies and Icing

gingerbread cookie dough
piping icing: light tan, dark tan,
  red, and light blue
flood icing: light tan and dark tan

Equipment and Embellishments

reindeer cutter
licorice shoelaces

Techniques

piping, flooding (pages 22, 24)
flooding on wet flood (page 24)
feathering dots (for tail) on wet
  flood (page 25)

1 Prepare, roll, and chill cookie dough according to recipe and rolling instructions.

2 Cut out two reindeer for each sleigh. Bake and cool according to recipe instructions.

3 Pipe and flood entire reindeer. While wet, carefully create antler, hoof, and spot details with dark tan flood. Dot flood on tail; draw toothpick toward tip of tail to create detail. Allow to dry completely. (This flood layer is optional, but gives detail depth).

4 Use dark tan piping icing to go over antler, hoof, tail, and spot details. Pipe nose and eye. Allow to dry.

5 Using piping icing, affix two licorice laces to back of sleigh cookie; attach one to each reindeer. Allow to dry.

MODERN TREES

The straight sides on these simple shapes are easy to pipe and flood, so they're great for beginning decorators. With just a few colors, you can achieve striking results.

Cookies and Icing
chocolate cookie dough
piping icing: light green
flood icing: light green, dark red,
  light red, and white

Equipment and
Embellishments
modern tree cutter

Techniques
piping, flooding (pages 22, 24)
flooding on wet flood (page 24)

1 Prepare, roll, and chill cookie dough according to recipe and rolling instructions.

2 Cut out tree shapes. Bake and cool according to recipe instructions.

3 Pipe and flood trees, leaving trunks bare. While icing is wet, make dots with contrasting flood icing. You can make contrasting dots overlap, or put one color in the center of another. Allow to dry.

easy

MRS. SANTA

Honor Santa's better half — the woman behind the man behind the toys — by creating her likeness in cookie form.

Cookies and Icing
gingerbread cookie dough
piping icing: white, red, blue, and
   black
flood icing: white and red

*Equipment and
Embellishments*
round cutter
flaked coconut

Techniques
piping, flooding (pages 22, 24)
piping googly eyes (page 23)
adding sugar sparkle (page 25)

1 Prepare, roll, and chill cookie dough according to recipe and rolling instructions.

2 Cut out round cookies. Bake and cool according to recipe instructions.

3 Pipe and flood hat. Pipe and flood base of white hair. Pipe eyes, nose, cheeks, and mouth. Allow all icing to dry.

4 Pipe and flood hatband and pom-pom. Sprinkle flaked coconut on wet icing. Pipe hair details. Allow to dry. Gently shake off excess coconut.

SUPER SPARKLY STAR

Cutouts are a great way to vary simple cookie shapes while keeping the decorating easy.

Cookies and Icing
chocolate cookie dough
piping icing: aqua
flood icing: aqua

Equipment and Embellishments
two star cutters, large and small
white sanding sugar
gold dragées

Techniques
making holes or cutouts (page 12)
piping, flooding (pages 22, 24)
adding sugar sparkle (page 25)
attaching candy add-ons
  (page 25)

1 Prepare, roll, and chill cookie dough according to recipe and rolling instructions.

2 Cut out large stars. Cut out smaller star in the middle of larger, aligning points. Bake and cool according to recipe instructions.

3 Pipe and flood. While wet, sprinkle with sanding sugar. Place dragées on points. Allow to dry. Gently shake off excess sugar.

easy

COOKIE CHRISTMAS CARDS

Friends and family will be thrilled to receive edible holiday greetings. A set of small letter cutters can wish "NOEL," "JOY," or "PEACE."

Cookies and Icing
gingerbread cookie dough
piping icing: light green, dark
  green, white, and red
flood icing: red

Equipment and
Embellishments
rectangle cutter
set of small letter cutters
mini and small snowflake cutters
small bell cutter
gold luster dust
clear spirits
small paintbrush
gold dragées

Techniques
making holes or cutouts (page 12)
piping, flooding (pages 22, 24)

1 Prepare, roll, and chill cookie dough according to recipe and rolling instructions.

2 Cut out rectangles. For cookie #1, cut out letters from rectangle; cut out one mini and one small snowflake for each rectangle. For cookie #2, cut out small bells. Bake all cookies and cool according to recipe instructions.

3 For #1, pipe lines on snowflakes. Pipe green outlines around letters, alternating dark and light color dots. Pipe white snowflake detail on rectangle. Allow to dry. Affix snowflakes to rectangle with piping icing. Allow to dry.

4 For #2, pipe and flood rectangle; allow to dry. While rectangle is drying, paint the bells with luster dust. Allow to dry. Pipe detail on bells. Affix cutout letters from cookie #1 and bells to rectangle with piping icing; allow to dry completely.

* **KEEP IT SIMPLE.** For cookie #2, affix letters and bells before baking (page 13), and skip piping and flooding the rectangle. Decorate bells as described.

PEPPERMINT TREAT

These cookies remind us of our favorite peppermint hard candies. The swirl effect looks impressive but is very easy to do.

Cookies and Icing
sugar cookie dough
piping icing: white
flood icing: white and red

Equipment and Embellishments
wrapped-candy cutter
toothpicks

Techniques
piping, flooding (pages 22, 24)
feathering stripes on wet flood
(page 25)

1 Prepare, roll, and chill cookie dough according to recipe and rolling instructions.

2 Cut out candy shapes. Bake and cool according to recipe instructions.

3 Pipe and flood entire cookie in white. While wet, create short lines from outside edge of round "candy" part of cookie, stopping a bit short of center (lines should look like the spokes of a wheel, with white in the middle). Starting from outside edge of one spoke, drag a toothpick through the lines in spiral pattern, continuing spiral into center. (In the photograph, the swirl begins just left of the 12 o'clock position. Follow the line around the cookie from there, and you'll see where your toothpick should go.) Allow to dry.

PRETTY PASTEL ORNAMENTS

People were known to have decorated their Christmas trees with sweets as early as the 16th century. With these simple, round-cutter ornaments, you can easily make a tree's worth of your own.

Cookies and Icing
sugar cookie dough
piping icing: yellow, light green, and red
flood icing: yellow, light green, and red

Equipment and Embellishments
round cutter
drinking straw
toothpicks
luster dust: silver and gold
clear spirits
small paintbrush
licorice shoelaces

Techniques
making holes or cutouts (page 12)
piping, flooding (pages 22, 24)
feathering dots (for hearts) on wet flood (page 25)
painting with luster dust (page 26)

1 Prepare, roll, and chill cookie dough according to recipe and rolling instructions.

2 Cut out ornament circles. Make holes on top of each ornament with straw. Bake and cool according to recipe instructions.

3 Pipe and flood ornaments.

4 For cookie #2, allow to dry. Paint luster dust stripes; allow to dry. Pipe yellow lines on luster dust. Allow to dry.

5 For cookie #1, while wet, make two lines of dots with red flood; draw toothpick through lines of dots to create hearts. Allow to dry. Paint gold luster dust stripes; allow to dry. Pipe tiny red dots around luster dust. Allow to dry.

6 Tie on licorice laces to hang ornaments.

EDIBLE GIFT TAGS

When the tag is this tasty, the recipient might be too busy eating the cookie to open the present!

Cookies and Icing
gingerbread cookie dough
piping icing: red
flood icing: red

Equipment and Embellishents
rectangle cutter
mini reindeer cutter
black food-safe marking pen

Techniques
piping, flooding (pages 22, 24)
writing with food-safe marking
  pens (page 26)

1   Prepare, roll, and chill cookie dough according to recipe and rolling instructions.

2   Cut out rectangles and one mini reindeer for each. Bake and cool according to recipe instructions.

3   Pipe and flood rectangle; allow to dry. Pipe nose on reindeer; draw eye with food-safe marking pen. Allow to dry.

4   With food-safe marking pen, write message on rectangle. Affix reindeer with piping icing; allow to dry.

THE MAN WITH THE BAG

Who doesn't love the right jolly old elf, especially when he's bearing a sackful of gifts? This image of Santa Claus was popularized in the 1820s by the now-famous poem "A Visit from Saint Nicholas" by Thomas Nast.

Cookies and Icing
sugar cookie dough
piping icing: red, white, and green
flood icing: red and white

Equipment and Embellishments
sideways Santa cutter
black sanding sugar
flaked coconut
gold dragées

Techniques
piping, flooding (pages 22, 24)
adding sugar sparkle (page 25)

1 Prepare, roll, and chill cookie dough according to recipe and rolling instructions.

2 Cut out Santa shapes. Bake and cool according to recipe instructions.

3 Pipe and flood Santa's suit and hat. Pipe and flood white bag and beard. Pipe green gift in bag. Allow to dry.

4 Pipe red outline detail on Santa, sleeve, and hat; pipe ribbon on gift. Allow to dry. Pipe belt and gloves in white; pipe and flood boots in white. While all are wet, sprinkle black sanding sugar on icing; allow to dry. Gently shake off excess black sugar.

5 Pipe cuff, hatband and pom-pom in white. While wet, sprinkle with coconut; allow to dry. Gently shake off excess coconut. Pipe eyes and nose; affix dragée buttons with red piping icing; allow to dry.

BEJEWELED CHRISTMAS TREE

No icing required for this stylized tree. A set of aspic cutters makes the jewel-colored dough ornaments that are placed on before baking.

Cookies and Icing
gingerbread cookie dough
sugar cookie dough: uncolored,
  blue, red, and green

*Equipment and
Embellishments*
paring knife or X-Acto blade
12-inch ruler
set of aspic cutters
gold luster dust
clear spirits
small paintbrush

Techniques
coloring dough (page 13)
adding dimension to cookies
  (page 13)
painting with luster dust
  (page 26)

1 Prepare, roll, and chill gingerbread cookie dough according to recipe and rolling instructions. Using a ruler, cut out triangles approximately 6 inches high from tip to bottom, with a 5½-inch base.

2 Prepare sugar cookie dough; divide dough and color. Roll and chill each color. Using aspic cutter, cut out one star for each triangle from the uncolored dough; place at top of the tree. Cut out ornaments from all colored doughs. Place ornaments on tree.

3 Bake and cool according to recipe instructions.

4 Paint star with luster dust; allow to dry.

easy

ICING-STENCILED ANGEL

A purchased stencil (see Resources) makes this intricate design a snap. On gingerbread, white icing makes a lovely contrast.

Cookies and Icing
gingerbread cookie dough
piping icing: white

Equipment and Embellishments
angel cutter with matching
  stencil
small offset spatula

Techniques
stenciling with icing (see step 3)

1 Prepare, roll, and chill cookie dough according to recipe and rolling instructions.

2 Cut out angels. Bake and cool according to recipe instructions.

3 Place stencil on cookie. Pipe or spread piping icing over stencil openings to lightly cover. Holding stencil in place, use a small offset spatula to smooth icing evenly over openings. Lift stencil straight up to avoid smearing. Allow to dry.

easy

TWO-TIERED STAR

You'll have Christmas stars in your eyes after you bite into the two delicious chocolate layers of this cookie sandwich.

Cookies and Icing
chocolate cookie dough
piping icing: green and white
flood icing: green

Equipment and Embellishments
3 star cutters in graduated sizes

Techniques
imprinting before baking
  (page 12)
piping, flooding (pages 22, 24)

1 Prepare, roll, and chill cookie dough according to recipe and rolling instructions.

2 For each cookie, cut out a large star and a midsized star. Before baking, imprint the center of the largest star with the smallest star, aligning the points. This will make a guide for icing. Using smallest cutter again, cut star completely out of the center of the midsized star, aligning points. Bake and cool according to recipe instructions.

3 Pipe and flood star shape on largest cookie, making star slightly larger than impressed lines. Allow to dry.

4 On back of midsized star, pipe a small amount of icing to each point. Affix to larger star so that points are aligned and green icing shows through.

5 Pipe decorative dots on the larger star, around the border of the smaller star. Allow to dry.

STANDING SNOWPEOPLE

With colorful scarves and easelbacks to make them stand, these smiling companions can be part of a winter wonderland tableau, or grace individual place settings. To make a place card, just use a food-safe marking pen to write your guests' names!

Cookies and Icing
cookie dough of your choice
piping icing: red, blue, and light green
flood icing: white, red, and light green

Equipment and Embellishments
snowperson cutter
square cutter
paring knife
sanding sugar: black and green

Techniques
piping, flooding (pages 22, 24)
adding sugar sparkle (page 25)
making stand-up cookies (page 26)

1 Prepare, roll, and chill cookie dough according to recipe and rolling instructions.

2 Cut out snowpeople. If your cutter has a rounded bottom, use a paring knife to trim flat bottoms. Cut out squares; cut squares in half diagonally with paring knife. These are your easelbacks. Bake and cool according to recipe instructions.

3 Pipe and flood snowpeople in white. While wet, sprinkle hat area with black sanding sugar. Allow to dry. Gently shake off excess sugar.

4 Pipe and flood scarf. (For cookie #2, sprinkle wet scarf with green sanding sugar, allow to dry, and gently shake off excess.) Pipe eyes and mouth; allow to dry.

5 Affix easelback to snowperson with piping icing. Allow to dry.

HOLLY-CUFFED STOCKING

Santa wouldn't hesitate to fill a stocking this adorable! Use your mighty toothpick to create the impressive holly design — it's really quite easy!

Cookies and Icing
sugar cookie dough
piping icing: red and light green
flood icing: red and dark green

Equipment and Embellishments
stocking cutter
toothpicks

Techniques
piping, flooding (pages 22, 24)
feathering short lines on wet flood
 (page 25)

1 Prepare, roll, and chill cookie dough according to recipe and rolling instructions.

2 Cut out stocking shapes. Bake and cool according to recipe instructions.

3 Pipe and flood entire stocking in red; allow to dry completely.

4 Pipe and flood stocking cuff in white. While wet, flood short dark green lines in V-shapes across cuff. Feather holly leaf lines by pulling toothpick from center of line outward, and from tips of lines outward. Allow to dry.

5 Pipe holly berries and light green dot details. Allow to dry.

SUGARY GLITTERY SNOWFLAKE

If you're dreaming of a white Christmas, why not bake up a batch of snowflakes? No two are alike — nature didn't imagine snowflake curlicues and swirls, but you can!

Cookies and Icing
chocolate cookie dough
piping icing: white

Equipment and Embellishments
snowflake cutter
white sanding sugar

Techniques
piping (page 22)
adding sugar sparkle (page 25)

1   Prepare, roll, and chill cookie dough according to recipe and rolling instructions.

2   Cut out snowflakes. Bake and cool according to recipe instructions.

3   Pipe snowflake design; while wet, sprinkle with sanding sugar. Allow to dry. Gently shake off excess sugar.

STAR OF WONDER, STAR OF LIGHT

Wise men and women will follow the candy windowpanes and sparkling sugar to the cookie plate!

Cookies and Icing
sugar cookie dough

Equipment and Embellishments
Star of the East cutter
small round cutter
small diamond cutter
red and green hard candies, crushed
sanding sugar: yellow and pink

Techniques
sugaring before baking (page 13)
making windowpanes (page 13)

1 Prepare, roll, and chill cookie dough according to recipe and rolling instructions.

2 Cut out stars. Cut out circles or diamonds in centers of cookies.

3 Before baking, sprinkle sanding sugar on cookie dough in a decorative pattern. Use a snack-size ziplock bag with a small corner cut out to control the flow of your sanding sugar. Add crushed hard candy to center hole. Bake and cool according to recipe instructions.

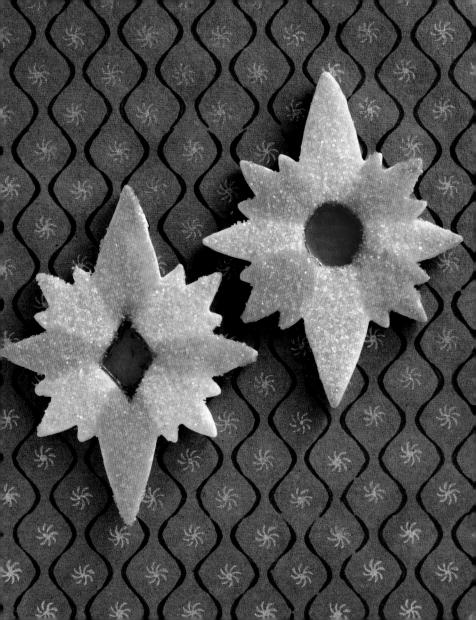

IT'S RAINING REINDEER!

Make a fleet of these bite-sized treats and bag them for party favors or bake sales. We dare you to eat just one!

Cookies and Icing
gingerbread cookie dough
piping icing: red

Equipment and Embellishments
mini reindeer cutter

Techniques
piping (page 22)

1 Prepare, roll, and chill cookie dough according to recipe and rolling instructions.

2 Cut out mini reindeer. Bake and cool according to recipe instructions.

3 Pipe red noses on reindeer.

✻ **KEEP IT SIMPLE.** If you don't want to make icing, sprinkle red nonpareils or red sanding sugar on the reindeer noses before baking.

easy

ROUND SNOWFLAKES

Three colors and a round cutter can make an afternoon full of whimsical fun. Once you get started, decorating a batch goes quickly — you'll wish you had doubled the recipe!

Cookies and Icing
cookie dough of your choice
piping icing: light blue and dark
    blue
flood icing: white, light blue, and
    dark blue

Equipment and
Embellishments
round cutter

Techniques
piping, flooding (pages 22, 24)
flooding on wet flood (page 24)

1   Prepare, roll, and chill cookie dough according to recipe and rolling instructions.

2   Cut out round cookies. Bake and cool according to recipe instructions.

3   Pipe and flood entire cookie. While wet, make snowflake design with contrasting flood icing. Allow to dry.

THE GIFT OF CHRISTMAS PRESENT

Who doesn't like surprise packages? This one comes wrapped in pretty icing stripes and is tied with a sparkly sugar bow!

Cookies and Icing
sugar cookie dough
piping icing: light green and red
flood icing: light green and red

Equipment and Embellishments
gift cutter
white sanding sugar

Techniques
piping, flooding (pages 22, 24)
flooding on wet flood (page 24)
adding sugar sparkle (page 25)

1 Prepare, roll, and chill cookie dough according to recipe and rolling instructions.

2 Cut out gift shapes. Bake and cool according to recipe instructions.

3 Pipe and flood entire cookie in light green; while wet, make stripes in red flood horizontally on gift box and vertically on lid. Allow to dry completely.

4 Pipe red stripes over flood stripes on gift box bottom; outline entire box and lid. Allow to dry.

5 Pipe and flood bow in red. While wet, sprinkle bow with sanding sugar; allow to dry. Gently shake off excess sugar.

SWEDISH DALA HORSE

The tradition of carving these horses began in the Swedish province of Dalarna as a way for woodcarvers to spend the long, dark winter nights. Still a prized handicraft, each horse exhibits the individuality of the carver — just as these cookies will show the individuality of the cookie crafter!

Cookies and Icing
gingerbread cookie dough
piping icing: red and blue
flood icing: red and light green

Equipment and Embellishments
Dala horse cutter
toothpicks
gold luster dust
clear spirits
small paintbrush
gold dragées

Techniques
piping, flooding (pages 22, 24)
feathering dots (for hearts) on
  wet flood (page 25)
painting with luster dust
  (page 26)

1 Prepare, roll, and chill cookie dough according to recipe and rolling instructions.

2 Cut out Dala horses. Bake and cool according to recipe instructions.

3 Pipe and flood entire horse red. While wet, flood dots for hooves, and create line of flood dots for mane and tail. Drag toothpick through dots from ear to saddle and saddle to tail to create hearts. Allow to dry.

4 Paint saddle with luster dust; allow to dry.

5 Affix gold dragées around saddle with red piping icing. Pipe on eye. Allow to dry.

✳ **KEEP IT SIMPLE.** To eliminate a drying step, add gold dragées to wet red flood icing before drying and painting saddle.

DELICATE CUT-OUT SNOWFLAKES

You can create an even greater variety of snowflakes by baking the cookies from the shapes you cut out of the centers!

Cookies and Icing
sugar cookie dough
piping icing: white

Equipment and Embellishments
various-sized snowflake cutters
luster dust: silver and blue
clear spirits
small paintbrush
multicolored dragées

Techniques
making holes or cutouts (page 13)
painting with luster dust
  (page 26)
attaching candy add-ons
  (page 25)

1   Prepare, roll, and chill cookie dough according to recipe and rolling instructions.

2   Cut out larger snowflakes; cut out smaller snowflake shapes from centers of larger snowflakes. Bake and cool according to recipe instructions.

3   Paint with silver or blue luster dust; allow to dry.

4   Affix dragées at points and corners with piping icing. Allow to dry.

STAND-UP TREE

Make a stand-up cookie forest with trees like this one!

Cookies and Icing
gingerbread cookie dough
piping icing: green and white
flood icing: green, blue, and red

Equipment and Embellishments
tree cutter
rectangle cutter
white sanding sugar
gold dragées

Techniques
piping, flooding (pages 22, 24)
flooding on wet flood (page 24)
adding sugar sparkle (page 25)
making stand-up cookies
   (page 26)

1 Prepare, roll, and chill cookie dough according to recipe and rolling instructions.

2 Cut out tree shapes. Cut out half as many rectangles as you have trees. Cut rectangles in half diagonally with paring knife. These are your easelbacks. Bake and cool completely.

3 Pipe and flood tree bodies with green icing. While wet, dot red and blue ornaments with wet flood. Allow to dry.

4 Pipe garland across tree. While garland is wet, sprinkle with sanding sugar; allow to set. Gently shake off excess.

5 Affix dragée to top of tree with piping icing. Affix easelback to tree with piping icing. Allow to dry.

WELCOMING HOLIDAY WREATH

A symbol borrowed from ancient times, the green circle of the wreath symbolizes the cycle of nature and the promise of rebirth. It's become a sign of welcome during the Christmas season.

Cookies and Icing
sugar cookie dough
piping icing: green and red

Equipment and Embellishments
round cutters, small and large
leaf pastry bag tip (such as #67)

Techniques
making holes or cutouts (page 12)
piping (page 22)
piping leaves (see below)

1 Prepare, roll, and chill cookie dough according to recipe and rolling instructions.

2 Cut out circles; cut smaller circles in center of larger ones to create wreath shape. Bake and cool according to recipe instructions.

3 Pipe overlapping leaves in one direction around wreath. Allow to dry. Pipe red berries. Allow to dry.

✳ **PIPING LEAVES.** If you've never piped leaves before, practice a few times on a sheet of waxed paper to get the hang of it. Remember, even real evergreens aren't perfect — it's part of their beauty!

Holding the flat side of the pastry bag tip against the cookie, exert pressure to form the flat end of the leaf. Ease off the pressure as you pull the tip toward you. The leaf should thin to form the pointed end.

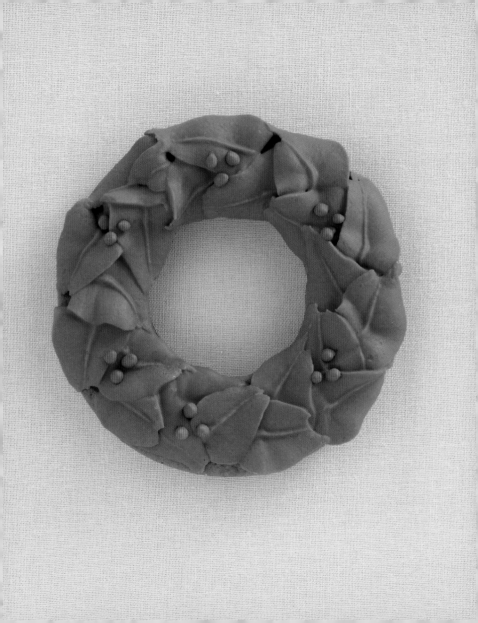

CORK-POPPING CHAMPAGNE!

Great for New Year's party favors, these edible champagne "bottles" are a happy, tasty way to ring in the new! Another option would be to write the coming year on the label.

Cookies and Icing
sugar cookie dough
piping icing: white and tan
flood icing: white and tan

Equipment and Embellishments
champagne bottle cutter
gold luster dust
clear spirits
small paintbrush
black food-safe marking pen

Techniques
piping, flooding (pages 22, 24)
painting with luster dust
  (page 26)
writing with food-safe marking
  pens (page 26)

1 Prepare, roll, and chill cookie dough according to recipe and rolling instructions.

2 Cut out champagne bottles. Bake and cool according to recipe instructions.

3 Pipe and flood tan base of label. Paint bottle neck with gold luster dust. Allow to dry.

4 Pipe and flood oval on label in white; pipe edges of label. Allow to dry.

5 Write *Happy New Year* (or other) message on label with food-safe marking pen.

HAPPY NEW YEAR NOISEMAKERS!

Making noise at midnight is an ancient tradition meant to drive bad luck away for the coming year. Use a candy cane cutter to make the familiar shape, and decorate in lively colors!

Cookies and Icing
sugar cookie dough
piping icing: red, tan, and white
flood icing: red, tan, cream, and
    white

*Equipment and
Embellishments*
candy cane cutter

Techniques
piping, flooding (pages 22, 24)
flooding on wet flood (page 24)

1   Prepare, roll, and chill cookie dough according to recipe and rolling instructions.

2   Cut out noisemaker shapes. Bake and cool according to recipe instructions.

3   For cookie #1, pipe and flood body of noisemaker (about halfway through "hook") in tan. While wet, make stripes running down the length of the cookie with cream flood icing. Allow to dry. Pipe red outline, dot detail, and "noise." Allow to dry.

4   For cookie #2, pipe and flood body of noisemaker in red. While wet, use white flood icing to make larger dots. Allow to dry. Pipe white dot detail around flooded dots; pipe outline on end; pipe "noise." Allow to dry.

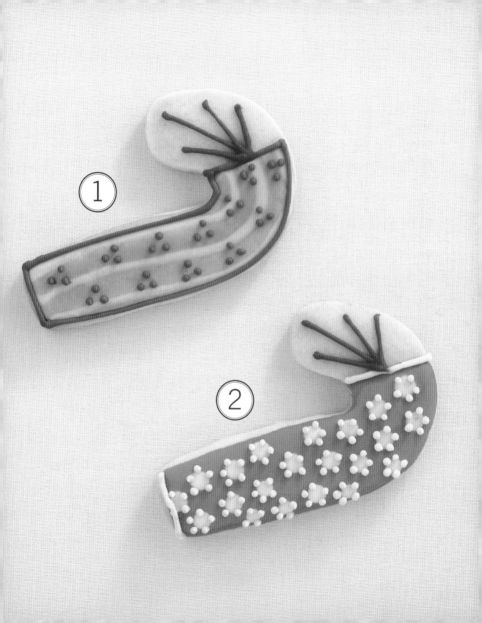

NYC'S NEW YEAR'S BALL DROP

. . . 5 . . . 4 . . . 3 . . . 2 . . . 1 . . . **Happy New Year! Make your own versions of the Times Square New Year's Eve icon and watch them drop into people's mouths!**

Cookies and Icing
sugar cookie dough
piping icing: white and various
  colors of choice

Equipment and Embellishments
round cutter
silver luster dust
clear spirits
small paintbrush

Techniques
piping (page 22)
painting with luster dust
  (page 26)

1 Prepare, roll, and chill cookie dough according to recipe and rolling instructions.

2 Cut out round cookies. Bake and cool according to recipe instructions.

3 Paint cookie with luster dust; allow to dry. Pipe lines to create grid on cookie; allow to dry.

4 Paint lines with luster dust; allow to dry. Pipe dots on intersections of lines; allow to dry.

COOKIES YOU CAN CREATE WITH A
ROUND CUTTER

Here are just some of the cookies you can create with a round cookie cutter.

MERRY CHRISTMAS

PART THREE

shipping &
party planning

shipping decorated cookies

We've never met anyone who doesn't like getting a box of delicious decorated cookies in the mail. Here's what we've learned about how to minimize breakage when we send our cookies out into the world.

1 Choose sturdy shapes with a minimum of thin appendages to reduce the danger of your cookies breaking en route.

2 Use tins to keep cookies fresh and help protect them. (See Resources.)

3 Make sure there's plenty of packing material inside the cookie tin:

 a Place a layer of crumpled waxed paper on the bottom of the tin.

 b Place another sheet of waxed paper in the tin, as if you were putting tissue paper in a gift box, but instead of making it neat, crumple it to fit against the sides of the tin.

 c Add your first layer of cookies. If you haven't individually wrapped them, fold each one in a small piece of waxed paper to keep them from jostling. Add small, crumpled pieces of waxed paper to any pockets of space to prevent cookie movement.

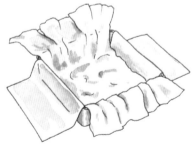

Crumpled waxed paper cushions the cookies

d Place another crumpled piece of paper on top of the packaged cookies, and then add another layer of cookies. Repeat until the tin is nearly full. Make sure the cookies lie flat and apart from each other and leave at least ¾ inch between the top layer of cookies and the top of the tin; add a fat top layer of protective padding (such as bubble cushioning or more crumpled waxed paper).

e Cover with the lid and gently shake the tin. If you feel no movement, shake it a little harder. If you feel movement, add more padding and do the "shake" test again until you feel no movement inside the tin.

f Attach your gift note to the top of the tin. Don't forget!

4 Make sure there's plenty of packing material between the tin and the box:

a Choose a box that allows at least 2 to 3 inches of space around the tin on all sides and above and below.

b Pad the bottom of the box with a healthy layer of packing peanuts, packing paper, or bubble cushioning.

c Place the cookie tin in the box, and thoroughly pad the space between the tin and the sides of the box.

d Pad the top tightly and close the box. Shake the package gently. If you feel no movement, shake it a little harder. If you feel movement, open the box and add more padding where needed, then close and seal the box, and ship.

Note: To help the environment, we reuse our packing materials — especially the nonrecyclable ones.

 cookie swap parties

Cookie swaps are fun at Christmastime — and they're a great way to ensure that you have a variety of cookies around the house, though you have to make only one type! The idea is that each guest brings a designated quantity of a cookie; the cookies are pooled, and each guest leaves with the same quantity he or she came with, but with a representative sampling of the cookies everyone brought. You can ask for only "Cookie Crafted" cookies or have guests contribute their own traditional favorites to mix and match.

GETTING READY FOR A SWAP

✱ What better way to invite people to a cookie swap than to put a photo of your own cookies on the invitation?

✱ Establish how many cookies each person should bring. Three dozen? Five dozen? Include this information on the invitation, and ask everyone to let you know what kind (or shape) of cookie they are decorating for the swap. (It's nice to avoid duplicates, but remember that the same cookies can look vastly different depending on each person's unique decorating flair.)

* Remind guests to bring copies of the recipes and/or a brief description of how the cookie is decorated, and let them know how many copies they should bring (based on the number of guests).

* Provide containers for each person to use to take home his or her cookie loot, or tell people to bring an extra container of their own. Pretty tins or boxes can serve as party favors. Inexpensive aluminum containers and baggies can also work as take-home packaging.

* Provide snacks and drinks so people won't be tempted to eat all the cookies they're supposed to be taking home (though of course, a few will disappear)!

IT'S PARTY TIME

* Arrange all the cookies on a table, with copies of the respective recipes near each one.

* If you're providing take-home containers or baggies, hand them out before the swap and let everyone know how many cookies to take of each variety on the table. To figure this out, divide the number of cookies each person has brought by the number of people attending the party. For example, if everyone brings three dozen cookies (36) and 15 people attend, each person takes home 2 of each variety of cookie (36 divided by 15 equals 2.4).

* If you have leftover cookies (those .4's!) your guests can either eat these along with the party treats you provide or take home an extra of their favorite cookie.

resources

This section lists where we got most of our cutters, but we've found that over the years, stocks change. We apologize if you can't find the exact cutter we use, but if you have your heart set on a certain shape and can't find it, you can get custom-designed cutters at CopperGifts.com. H. O. Foose Tinsmithing even sells a kit that allows you to make your own.

A. C. Moore, Hobby Lobby, JoAnn's Fabrics & Crafts, Michael's

These and other craft stores carry a wide range of baking and decorating supplies, and we get our cookie slats in the craft aisle.

Ateco

www.atecousa.com
Ateco offers a wide line of baking and decorating products. This is the source for aspic cutters.

The Baker's Catalogue

www.kingarthurflour.com
This site carries our favorite item: parchment sheets that exactly fit a half-sheet pan.

Broadway Panhandler

www.broadwaypanhandler.com
866-266-5927
A New York institution for cookware and baking supplies.

Candyland Crafts

www.candylandcrafts.com
877-487-4289
A source for candy embellishments, such as dragées, candy pearls, and eyes.

Chef Central

www.chefcentral.com
201-576-0100 (Paramus, NJ) and
914-328-1375 (Hartsdale, NY)
They have a huge selection and good prices.

The Container Store

www.containerstore.com
Carries a wide variety of wrapping and packing materials.

The Cookie Cutter Shop

www.cookiecuttershop.com
A large selection of metal cutters.

A Cook's Companion

197 Atlantic Avenue, Brooklyn, NY 11201
718-852-6901
This lovely and well-stocked store is in Janice's neighborhood in Brooklyn.

Cookietins.com

www.cookietins.com
A great source for tins of all sizes and other cookie-packing accessories.

CopperGifts.com

www.coppergifts.com
Copper cutters (including custom), and other cookie supplies, including the kit to make the icing-stenciled angel on page 130.

Country Kitchen Sweet Art

www.countrykitchensa.com
800-497-3927
We got elf, poinsettia, and pinecone cutters here, as well as candy "lay-on" embellishments, such as mini Santa faces.

The Great American Spice Company

www.americanspice.com
A great source of 1-pound bags of sanding sugar in a variety of colors at great prices.

H. O. Foose Tinsmithing Co.

www.foosecookiecutters.com
A huge selection of inexpensive cutters.

Kitchen Collecibles

http://kitchengifts.com
A source of copper cookie cutters and other cookie-making supplies.

Kitchen Krafts

www.kitchenkrafts.com
The food crafter's supply catalog.

Off the Beaten Path

www.cookiecutter.com
Cutters at reasonable prices.

Sur La Table

various locations and online at
www.surlatable.com
Well-stocked for bakers.

Sweet Celebrations

www.sweetc.com
Baking-supplies catalog carries festive twist ties and sticks for cookie pops.

Wilton

www.wilton.com
They have good prices for cellophane bags.

other storey titles
you will enjoy

250 Treasured Country Desserts, by Andrea Chesman &
Fran Raboff.
A nostalgic collection of more than 250 recipes for home bakers
to rely on for all occasions.
416 pages. Paper. ISBN 978-1-60342-152-2.

The Baking Answer Book, by Lauren Chattman.
Answers every question about common and specialty ingredients,
the best equipment, and the science behind the magic of baking.
384 pages. Flexibind. ISBN 978-1-60342-439-4.

Cookie Craft, by Valerie Peterson & Janice Fryer.
Clear instruction, practical methods, and all the tips and tricks for
beautifully decorated special occasion cookies.
168 pages. Hardcover. ISBN 978-1-58017-694-1.

Ghoulish Goodies, by Sharon Bowers.
A colorful collection of creepy treats for celebrating Halloween or
any frightful occasion.
160 pages. Paper. ISBN 978-1-60342-146-1.

These and other books from Storey Publishing are available
wherever quality books are sold or by calling 1-800-441-5700.
Visit us at *www.storey.com.*